WRESTLING COACH'S SURVIVAL GUIDE

Practical Techniques and Materials for Building an Effective Program and a Winning Team

KEITH T. MANOS

PARKER PUBLISHING COMPANY
West Nyack, NY 10995

10 9 8 7 6 5 4 3 2 1

Library of Congress Cataloging-in-Publication Data

Manos, Keith T.
    Wrestling coach's survival guide / Keith T. Manos ; photographs by Donna Zitel.
        p. cm.
    ISBN 0-13-458951-3
    1. Wrestling—Coaching—Handbooks, manuals, etc. I. Title.
    GV1196.3.M35   1996
    796.8`12—dc20   95-37234
                                                                                         CIP

ISBN 0-13-458951-3

Parker Publishing Company
West Nyack, NY 10995

A Simon & Schuster Company

Printed in the United States of America

DEDICATION

For my father, who taught me anything is possible, and my wrestlers,
who proved he was right.

ACKNOWLEDGMENTS

This book exists due to the efforts of athletes across the country, their parents, their coaches, and their school administrators. All contributed their opinions on the qualities of an effective wrestling coach. To them, I am grateful. I must also acknowledge editor Connie Kallback whose commitment to this project was as intense as the championship match of a state wrestling tournament. She has been a great coach for me.

Photos by Donna Zitel, Kirtland, Ohio.

ABOUT THE AUTHOR

Keith Manos has published many nonfiction coaching/teaching articles in national publications like ATHLETIC MANAGEMENT, SCHOLASTIC COACH, SCHOOL LIBRARY JOURNAL, STRATEGIES (A Journal for Physical and Sport Educators), DFA SPORTS JOURNAL, HICALL, and WRESTLING USA.

He is currently an English teacher at Richmond Heights (OH) High School and has coached wrestling over 17 years at four different high schools. His coaching experiences have been with athletes as young as six and as old as twenty-six. In 1993-94, he served as an assistant wrestling coach at Cuyahoga Community College in Cleveland, Ohio.

His "Seminar for Successful Coaching" has been conducted at several colleges and high schools, and he has been a clinician at over forty wrestling camps in his coaching tenure. He has been the head coach for numerous all star wrestling teams, including the 1989 USA All Star Team which competed against the Oklahoma All Stars and the 1991 Ohio All-Star Wrestling Team which traveled and competed in several western states. Over sixty of Keith's athletes have earned all state or all conference honors.

Keith's other awards include:

☑ Ohio Wrestling Coach of the Year (1988)

☑ Greater Cleveland Division III Wrestling Coach of the Year (1989)

☑ East Suburban Conference Coach of the Year (1988, 1989)

☑ NE Division III Coach of the Year (1989)

Over thirty of Keith's wrestlers have competed in the Ohio State Wrestling Tournament during his 14 years as a head wrestling coach. Three won individual state titles while 16 others placed in the top six. Six times his teams finished in the top ten (out of nearly 200 schools).

In 1993 Keith earned a Master's Degree in English (Creative Writing) from Cleveland State University. His skill as a teacher of writing has enabled him to serve as an editor of various educational newsletters and student publications. Currently, Keith is marketing a novel about high school wrestling while he continues to do freelance writing. His other articles appeared in publications like FULL-TIME DADS, LUTHERAN JOURNAL, NEW EARTH REVIEW, and VISIONS.

Keith is also a well-known motivational speaker for civic organizations, athletic teams, and awards programs in the Cleveland area when he isn't spending time with his wife and four-year-old daughter.

ABOUT THIS BOOK

Coaching wrestling remains an extremely difficult task. Administrators demand that we manage all paperwork and equipment efficiently and professionally; parents routinely expect their sons to emerge as dynamic and competitive athletes at every match; and our wrestlers especially test our patience and endurance. Dealing successfully with these responsibilities, pressures, and relationships is the core of *Wrestling Coach's Survival Guide*.

As a coach, you have to recognize first that championship coaching in any sport requires championship commitment. Many coaches translate commitment into a weekly routine of long hours, repetitive practices, tense competitions, and daily exhaustion. But it doesn't have to be that way. A coaching contract guarantees your duty to the school; your commitment guarantees a promise to the wrestlers, a promise to bring your passion and diligence into the practice room and devotion and friendship into their lives.

Wrestling Coach's Survival Guide is an informative and constructive book for junior high school, senior high school, and college coaches who want more from their teams than they're getting. The coach who reads this book can find in clear and concise language the practical and specific strategies that can create competitive teams composed of motivated wrestlers. *Wrestling Coach's Survival Guide* teaches you how to save time, lessen stress, inspire wrestlers, involve the community, handle paperwork, and create championships (for yourself and especially for your kids).

From pep talks to publicity, pre-season to post-season, *Wrestling Coach's Survival Guide* offers fresh advice and innovative methods that even the most veteran coaches can find useful. It is designed to empower any coach with the skills required in training today's wrestlers whether they're remarkably talented or hopelessly unskilled. *Wrestling Coach's Survival Guide* will assist you in organizing a competitive program and help broaden your understanding of wrestling (and the entire coaching process).

What makes this book special is that it provides information from your most important sources: wrestlers ages 12-22, coaches from all levels, parents in various communities, administrators at both the secondary school and college levels, and sports psychologists who explain their views on what makes an effective, successful wrestling coach. These interviews and the research gleaned from periodicals and texts offer outstanding and insightful commentary about coaching wrestling today.

Readers can expect details about the following:

- ☑ What does it take to be a successful wrestling coach?
- ☑ Creating a personal philosophy for coaching wrestling—What's at stake for you?
- ☑ The appeal of winning—How strong is it?
- ☑ Evaluating your coaching style—Is it more fluff than stuff?
- ☑ Letting wrestlers "own" the team
- ☑ Setting goals—Each day, each week, each season
- ☑ Why some kids stay, why some quit
- ☑ Dealing with pressure and how to stay off the emotional roller coaster
- ☑ Getting wrestlers to commit themselves to the program

- ☑ Successful networking—How to involve alumni and others
- ☑ The Winning way to wrestle-offs
- ☑ Your wrestler, their child—Dealing successfully with parents
- ☑ Motivating your wrestlers
- ☑ Publicizing your wrestlers
- ☑ Duties of the head coach and assistant coaches
- ☑ The coach and the official—Staying right with the referee
- ☑ The five W's of successful practices
- ☑ Organizing your time, talent, and team
- ☑ Drills and skills for success
- ☑ Preparing for a competition—Fright, fight, or "psych"
- ☑ Achievement is in the eye of the beholder
- ☑ Budgets and bureaucracy—Working with your athletic director
- ☑ Don't get burned by burn-out

Generally, coaches hear only the opinions of their own wrestlers (if at all), the wrestlers' parents (possibly after a match, possibly not at all), or their school administrators (often by memorandum only). *Wrestling Coach's Survival Guide* contains clear insights and practical advice from successful coaches, concerned athletes, veteran officials, supportive administrators, sports psychologists, and community members from across the country presented in a simple, non-threatening way. This book can benefit all coaches who want their coaching experiences to be rewarding regardless of the size of the school community, its athletic tradition, or their won/loss record.

Wrestling Coach's Survival Guide also contains over thirty sample forms and letters which are ready for duplication and immediate use. They enable you to simplify your paperwork, organize any practice, and publicize your program.

Wrestling is a highly individualized sport, and just as there are a hundred techniques available for wrestlers to use in their matches there are a hundred coaching styles for coaches to use with their teams. This book will enhance your coaching style and offer specific strategies to help you avoid the mistakes and obstacles that await you every time you step on the mat. It will stimulate your creativity and help improve your relationships with your wrestlers. *Wrestling Coach's Survival Guide* is my contribution to the wrestling community and especially my fellow coaches who teach the sporting world the oldest and greatest sport.

CONTENTS

Section 4   **Motivation 67**

Section 5   **The Coach's Duties 87**

SECTION 1

A Philosophy for Coaching

When their teenagers take the plunge into competitive sports, parents often expect the coach to be a special surrogate parent figure who can motivate like Vince Lombardi, teach like Socrates, and win like Dan Gable. Such high expectations can make even the most confident person uncertain about becoming a wrestling coach. Yet, in truth, we enjoy that challenge.

We're willing to accept the heavy responsibility of coaching other adults' children in return for a reward that we envision awaits us at the end of the season. For some of us, the reward has to be a winning season; others need only a simple, yet sincere, "Thanks, Coach. I couldn't have done it without you." But there is more to coaching than championship teams and grateful athletes. Whatever you expect to get from being a wrestling coach depends in large measure on what you expect from yourself.

A school has its mission statement. A corporation has a company policy. A coach needs his personal philosophy. You can call it your personal beliefs or professional standards or private credo; it doesn't matter as long as you have one.

Just like parents who raise their children in the same manner that they were raised, coaches often adopt the coaching style of the man who coached them. "I tried to coach like my high school coach (National Wrestling Hall of Fame Member Mike Milkovich of Maple Heights, Ohio) by being organized and disciplined," says Frank Romano, assistant wrestling coach at Kent State University. I thought it was the best way I could give back to the sport that has done so much for me as a person. I love being around young people. It keeps you alive and gives you purpose."

Anyone who chooses to coach wrestling needs to have strong reasons to do so. These reasons form the foundation of a philosophy that guides that coach through every decision he makes about his program. To formulate that philosophy the coach has to list his priorities.

1

WHAT ARE YOUR PERSONAL PRIORITIES?

*"A man can be as great as he wants to be. If
you believe in yourself and have the courage, the
determination, the dedication, the competitive
drive and if you are willing to sacrifice the
little things in life and pay the price for the
things that are worthwhile, it can be done."*

—(FROM VINCE LOMBARDI)

Your philosophy need not be profound, nor does it have to be extensive. Determining your philosophy of coaching, however, does require a brutal honesty and a self-reflection that most coaches avoid. They avoid this because it can be uncomfortable to document the beliefs that stand behind the way they coach. They might discover that the desire to win matches dominates the impulse to help kids. Or, they simply hate admitting that they have no philosophy at all. Having a clear personal philosophy, however, is crucial to being a coach.

Your philosophy should, in fact, be your top priority for successful coaching. Through every season, you will come to depend more on your coaching philosophy than any other skill or talent you may have as a coach. That is why it should be based on sound principles and strong beliefs.

It is probably best to list those beliefs in writing. As times change you should review and possibly update them. You should be prepared, in fact, to modify your philosophy if a change can help you and your wrestlers.

For many of us, that personal philosophy has developed through our own experiences as athletes. I was a mediocre high school wrestler, and my losses often left me embarrassed and depressed. When I began coaching I still lived with those losses, so individual achievement for my athletes was very important to me. I wanted them to discover the pleasure and rewards that seemed to come with winning. I didn't want them to miss that as I had. My first philosophy, therefore, was grounded in a single statement: "Everything I do is designed to help the kids win."

As the years passed and my experience as a coach grew, my philosophy took on weight:

"The kids win with class and dignity."

"The kids win with class and dignity. They must earn the respect of their opponents while striving to do their best."

"The kids will always work their hardest to be successful. They will do this in a dignified, respectful, and competitive manner."

What will be your foundation? Howard Ferguson, legendary Ohio wrestling coach whose St. Edwards High School teams won eleven state titles, offers this caution to coaches: "The next time you're getting ready to play a game, ask yourself why you're playing. A game is not supposed to be work. It's not something you have to do . . . Do it for fun. Do it because you want to do it. Practice is the hard part; the game should be fun . . . Stop worrying about winning and losing. If you've prepared right, you shouldn't have to worry."

Whatever you do, the match should always belong to the wrestler. After you recognize this, you need to make a powerful decision about your philosophy, and often that decision needs to address the attitude you have about winning and losing.

WINNING VS. LOSING—WHAT'S AT STAKE?

Vince Lombardi said: "It is a reality of life that men are competitive and the most competitive games draw the most competitive men. That's why they are here—to compete. The object is to win fairly, squarely, by the rules—but to win." Charlie Brown said: "Winning ain't everything, but losing is nothing."

Wins and losses too often are the basic tenant for judging any athletic program whether it's a junior high team or a Division I college program. But there are other ways of addressing this question:

Is victory special if dignity is sacrificed?

Does losing hurt as much if respect is gained?

What's at stake for the coach and, in turn, for the wrestler?

How important is winning to the coach?

How damaging is losing?

How much is the coach (or the wrestler) willing to risk to gain a victory?

"I like a coach who always pushes his team to their full potential but isn't so bent on winning that he forgets we're human."

—(FROM A HIGH SCHOOL WRESTLER)

Janet Spence, a University of Texas professor who studied 4000 employees and students, found that the most competitive people feel the most isolated, are the most wary of others, and are the most likely to maintain a distance from their peers.

Spence's study does not suggest that coaches adopt an anti-competition attitude, but it does indicate that coaches should examine their own competitiveness before training athletes. Certainly there is no joy in losing. A loss in any form can be crushing, but in athletics rarely is it the end. Learning how to handle a setback, a hardship, or a loss prepares young people for the difficulties outside athletics. Winning and losing is a time of discovery.

"As teachers and coaches, we must remember that when mere winning is our only goal, we are doomed to disappointment and failure. But when our goal is to try to win, when our focus is on preparation and

sacrifice and effort instead of on numbers on a
scoreboard then we will never lose."

—(FROM MIKE KRZYZEWSKI, DUKE UNIVERSITY)

It is not uncommon for a coach, especially a very competitive one, to be tempted to abandon his principles because of the pressure to win. "We do not want a coach who wants to win at all cost," says Louis Pronga, athletic director at Illinois Valley Central High School. "The coach should be a good role model who teaches by example. Winning is not a factor in how we hire a coach. It's more important that we get someone who has professional ethics and commitment. Sports is only one part of the educational process." Joe Paterno of Penn State recognizes that "it is always good to know what it is to lose. I guess it means that we've got to get back to work."

Sports gives young people an opportunity to strive for excellence, to risk losing in order to learn, and to grow into successful people. Winning at wrestling should not be the end of their goal-setting, it should be only the beginning.

"Winning and losing are both very temporary
things. Having done one or the other, you move
ahead. Gloating over a victory or sulking over
a loss is a good way to stand still."

—(FROM CHUCK KNOX, NFL COACH)

HOW CAN COACHING BE AN EMOTIONAL ROLLERCOASTER?

When coaches focus their program on the number of wins produced by the season's end, they are setting themselves up to ride an emotional rollercoaster. That's the bad news. The good news is that you don't have to buy a ticket. If you get too pumped up about winning and too depressed about losing, you can find yourself riding the gut-wrenching peaks and valleys of a rollercoaster track. This can not only be an emotional nightmare, but, it's also unhealthy.

As a former coach in the NFL, Sam Rutigliano has seen all the highs and lows of coaching. Currently the head football coach at Liberty University, Rutigliano sees the way to a rewarding career through finding "a middle level." He warns that "a lot of good men become Jekyll and Hydes and everyone they touch suffers."

So keep an even keel. Don't get too excited about winning or too disappointed with a loss. Your wrestlers need to see a coach who maintains his composure and poise no matter who wins the competition.

CAN FUN + FUNDAMENTALS = A FOUNDATION AND A FUTURE?

Concentrate on having fun, teaching the fundamentals, and building the self-esteem of your wrestlers. Your better athletes will always find a way to win regardless of the amount of emphasis that is placed on victory, and your less-skilled wrestlers will find the sport to be rewarding.

Be creative and make practices fun as well as challenging. Make sure the wrestlers learn the fundamentals of the sport so that they can execute them correctly during any competition. And always convey an optimistic outlook about the season, the team, and the individuals. In this way, your wrestlers' memories of you as their coach will be positive ones. Competing under you will have been a satisfying experience, something they can then share with the wrestlers that follow them.

Some caution, however, is needed here. As you work at the fundamentals with your team and try to create a pleasant yet challenging environment for your wrestlers, you need to evaluate the personal relationship you form with them. The best guideline here is to respect each wrestler's individuality and background, just as you would have them respect yours. A stern, formal approach and a loose, intimate association are the two extremes to be avoided.

When determining your personal coaching philosophy, consider the priorities your administration has. "The coach we hire must have a solid value system that places importance on kindness to others and on hard work to achieve quality," says Richmond Heights High School principal Dr. Hans Pesch. "The individual must show genuine care for their athletes and know how to teach that attitude to them." Determining a philosophy also means establishing goals.

WHY SET GOALS FOR THE TEAM, THE WRESTLER, AND YOURSELF?

Goals are essential. If designed correctly, they keep everyone on the same path and headed in the same direction. Again, they might be phrased in terms like "Win the league." "Make it to the state tournament." "Go undefeated."

There are other goals, maybe more important ones, that need to be addressed. When goals are created based only on racking up wins, a serious error is made. Goals, in fact, could have nothing to do with winning. Goals first need to be created by the team as a whole. Second, they should focus on what the wrestlers can *do*. Finally, they should be phrased in terms of positive outcomes. For example, the first goal below is phrased incorrectly while the second expresses the goal in better terminology:

1. We will not commit any penalties against _____ High School.

2. We will wrestle a penalty-free match against _____ High School.

Moreover, goals and objectives need to be based on (1) the amount of time you will have the wrestlers under your direction, (2) the difficulty of the skills they need to master, (3) why they have chosen to compete in wrestling, (4) their level of commitment and maturity, and (5) how much they are willing to contribute to others on the team.

Put goals in terms of what you want the wrestlers **to do**. For example, a team goal may be to increase by 50 percent the number of takedowns in the next match, or to have everyone complete a sub-six minute mile run, or to increase the total amout of poundage on the bench press. Avoid goals like "Dominate our opponent" or "To do our best," which are often vague and do not relate to the actual amount of effort you want the athletes to exert.

The competitions in the early season can be considered as intense training sessions, as valuable learning experiences, and as stepping stones to the tournaments at the end of the season. Unfortunately, too many coaches feel threatened by early-season losses and too many wrestlers see them as indicators of their entire season. The most important goals reflect what the individual wrestlers and the coaching staff want to accomplish by the **end** of the season. Everything before that should be seen as competitive training sessions that offer valuable experiences.

Emphasize to wrestlers the importance of establishing goals and, of course, involve them in the formation of those goals. They need to see that having goals is helpful, that they add a competitive challenge for the squad and prompt a better work ethic. Goals enable coaches to check progress and provide challenges. This is particularly important for those wrestlers who need frequent and achievable objectives to make training enjoyable.

Meaningful goals should:

☑ prioritize the health of the wrestlers;

☑ educate the athletes about the value of hard work, cooperation, self-discipline, and commitment;

☑ promote an enjoyment of wrestling;

☑ empower wrestlers to set individual goals;

☑ foster a desire to be successful;

☑ demand that the school be represented in a respectful and dignified manner;

☑ promote a successful relationship with parents, the community and the school administration; and

☑ encourage victory in competitions.

The coaching staff should not set all the goals alone. All members of the team must be involved here. The group has to operate with one positive direction—for example, "Be league champions"—which should be clarified either at the beginning or end of every practice until the goal has been accomplished. These goals must be sound, reasonable, and reachable.

Be sure that every wrestler feels that he is making a strong contribution to the team goals. No one, including your assistant coach, should feel that he is only along for the ride, that his input or effort doesn't really count, or that the superstars are the only ones helping the team be successful. The team's success depends on many factors, but it certainly has to be important to your wrestlers to be on your team. They have to see that all their effort is for a worthwhile purpose.

Goals are challenges: They are a means of making the coaches and the wrestlers' efforts purposeful. They are essential for any program. David Hemery analyzed the importance of goals established cooperatively between the coach and players in his book *The Pursuit of Sporting Excellence*. "The mutual effort towards a common goal," writes Hemery, "brings a closeness and sharing and this enhances communication. This makes the process valuable in itself, regardless of the outcome."

Before you can discuss goals with your wrestlers, you need to have a more private discussion. This one is with yourself. You need to discover the goals you want to accomplish—goals so important, in fact, that you will not procrastinate, relax, or quit until they are accomplished. Maintain a positive attitude and a clear focus on those goals.

Later, talk to assistants, athletes, administrators, and even the parents. Get their input. No athletic program can function effectively without specific goals. "Common goals, similar attitudes, mutual respect—that's what creates a successful season," says Rex Holman, who won a national championship his senior year for Ohio

State University. The same results can happen for your team if you set meaningful goals, develop an organized plan of action, and follow through with passion and diligence.

WHY COACH?

According to a survey done at six Kansas universities, coaches identified three main reasons for entering into the coaching profession. They said they coach because they

1. enjoy working with young people;

2. have a strong interest in the sport; and

3. enjoy the professional and competitive challenge.

There are other reasons not identified by these Kansas coaches. According to an informal survey, coaches indicated that they coach because they

☑ enjoy being in the media and receiving the attention of the public;

☑ enjoy the social interactions that take place with fellow coaches, school staff, and the athletes;

☑ seek to advance in the profession—junior high to high school, then high school to college;

☑ do it for the fun and satisfaction of working with young wrestlers and assisting in their growth; and

☑ be simply excited about producing winning teams.

For me, teaching just wasn't enough. As a coach, I can see a whole new side of my students. Coaching provides the special experience of reaching each wrestler's heart as well as his mind. Bill McGrain, a football and wrestling coach at Olmsted Falls High School in Ohio, chose to coach for the "love of athletics, the competition, and the respect you get from the athletes. When they graduate, you can see your influence in their success. It's especially wonderful when former wrestlers return years later and are genuinely pleased to see me."

Your reasons may compare to these, or you may have other motivations for choosing to coach young people. Whatever your reasons for entering the coaching profession, your task is a huge one. You are making a profound decision when you decide to make a contribution to a young person's life. Such an impact cannot be taken lightly.

You should expect to be judged for what you say, do, and accomplish. You may receive criticism when you expect praise and suffer defeat when victory seemed assured. Overcoming such obstacles is the basis for effective coaching. That's the true challenge that draws most of us to this wonderful profession. We ask: "Can I be successful?"

To answer, if you have perseverance and a positive attitude, you probably can. We all need to model these traits for our kids. Simply, coaching is teaching, and the best coaches are often the best teachers.

So ask yourself: Why do I want to coach? I ask myself this before and after every season. Sometimes, days pass before my answer is complete. Any doubts, however, dissipate when I walk that school hallway and hear, "Hey, Coach" from my students. Somehow, their dual acknowledgement of my presence and profession provides a great feeling, a profound boost for my sometimes fragile ego. I return the greeting always with a smile.

> *"Having a group of student athletes respect me as a person . . . having past players visit or send letters. I can tell they are successful, team-minded, and well-rounded individuals. They know how to achieve. My athletes are my greatest achievements."*
>
> —(FROM AN OHIO COACH)

As coaches, we are given a tremendous opportunity to make a positive impact on our wrestlers. Wrestling enables young men of all shapes and sizes to participate in a physically demanding, highly competitive sport that stresses team accomplishments while offering participants the chance for individual achievement in tournament competition. Kids learn how to work hard and make positive decisions. They grow from being dependent boys to independent young men. Coaching them can be great fun, but there's much we need to learn to make it that way.

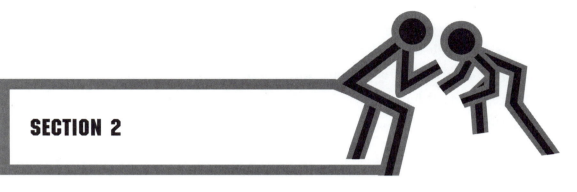

SECTION 2

The Coach-Wrestler Relationship

Vince Lomardi said: *"Individual commitment to a group effort—that is what makes a team work, a company work, a society work, a civilization work."*

TEACHING WRESTLERS TO MAKE A COMMITMENT

Most coaches agree that you don't win with the techniques you know, you win with the athletes you teach. Clearly, the wrestler's physical talent and personal commitment become crucial elements in both individual and team success. A coach may not be able to alter wrestlers' talents, but he can do something about their level of commitment.

Let's take for granted that the deeper the commitment, the greater the achievement. But how can a coach teach athletes to become more committed to the team and the program?

First, coaches have to recognize that each wrestler begins the season with a different level of commitment, a different reason for competing, and a different relationship with the coaching staff. The coach should discover how committed each athlete is, define the level of commitment he feels is necessary for team success, and, consequently, work to improve the athletes' commitment.

How? Have a private conversation with the wrestler to find out how committed he is. It is best to do this before the season even begins, possibly during a free period at school or over the telephone. If you cannot accomplish it then be sure to talk to the wrestler before or after practice during the first week of the season. Ask the athlete: "What are you willing to do this year to make yourself and the team successful?"

Don't get upset or dismayed if their answers aren't dynamic descriptions of the great sacrifices they plan to make. Indeed, many kids, especially the younger ones, may respond with, "I don't know." You probably will be the first coach ever to ask them this. That is when you need to define commitment for them. Explain that committed wrestlers:

1. do not break training rules;

2. are goal-oriented (both team and individual);

3. are punctual for practices, meetings, and competitions;

4. attend all practices;

5. maintain enthusiasm and intensity during practice;

6. encourage teammates to make improvements;

7. enjoy challenges and work hard to accomplish them;

8. are dedicated and reliable;

9. are coachable and cooperative; and

10. are responsible students in the classroom.

When you discuss commitment with a wrestler, it is best to describe an athlete who demonstrates these characteristics. You can also offer an example of a previous wrestler on the team who exemplified commitment. Often, the committed wrestler expects to arrive early and stay late, maintains a positive attitude especially during a crisis (losing the "big" match, for example), and anticipates success, not failure, before competitions.

You can even use a chart on a chalk board to simplify the teaching of commitment:

1———-2———-3———-4———-5———-6———-7———-8———-9———-10
Low Level   Average Level   High Level

The use of numbers can sometimes clarify commitment for kids, just as they would recognize the impact that 80 miles per hour has over 40 miles per hour in a car.

Kids with low levels (1-3) typically arrive one minute before practice begins and leave one second after you've dismissed them. Wrestling may be secondary for them (they're participating, for instance, only to stay in shape for football). They may not show much aggressiveness in competitions or much emotion about success or failure.

Their lack of commitment need not be criticized. In time, they can be motivated to work toward higher levels. "An effective coach for me," says Kent Huxel, a varsity wrestler at Cleveland Heights High School in Ohio, "pushes me to the limit. It's someone who is dedicated, who gives you encouragement, but also pushes you to the next level."

Identifying wrestlers with average levels of commitment (4-7) can be frustrating for a coach. Often, these athletes are uncertain whether they should do more or less. They give medium effort at practice and have average success at competitions. They always listen to the coach at practice but may lose their focus at a crucial moment in a match.

Once again, hold off on the criticism. Teach them first how intensifying their commitment can benefit both the team and themselves. This kind of sacrifice doesn't happen easily. You need to develop a sound relationship with each individual both on and off the mat. If disagreements and questions occur, it's essential that the wrestlers not only respect and trust your judgments, but also know you're very interested in them as individuals.

What kind of wrestler matches up to numbers 8–10? This kid practices hard and then runs at night. He is eager to learn and loves to compete. The coach may see that this wrestler is the first to congratulate or console a teammate after a match. This type of athlete never complains no matter what the circumstances. In short, he creates his own success.

You cannot judge commitment by wins and losses, and commitment is truly characterized by actions, not by talk. It may be appealing to hear an athlete say, "I am committed to being a state champion," but a better statement would be, "I am committed to **practicing and competing** like a state champion."

Commitment surfaces in what the athlete is willing **to do**. A statement like "I plan to give it all I've got" does little to indicate commitment. Better statements, like the ones below, clarify the actions, attitude, and behavior necessary for high level commitment:

—"I am committed to practice with intensity and alertness."

—"I am committed to learning all I can, following the coach's directions, and always making weight so the team doesn't have to forfeit."

—"I'm committed to practicing, learning, and acting like a state champ."

You may begin by discussing effective vs. ineffective statements of commitment. Help your wrestlers verbalize their commitment in terms of what they will do, not what they want to have happen. Again, don't become discouraged if you find that the younger guys are not be willing to do very much. Engage them in making a single commitment like increasing their total pushups in a single practice from 50 to 100, then to 150.

Next, talk about the great athletes (even those from other sports) who were highly committed. If available, show videotapes of these individuals and comment on their intensity. You can also use videotapes of matches and practices where wrestlers performed with intensity and desire, enabling you to point out examples of enthusiasm and perseverance.

As your season progresses, give an informal weekly progress report to each athlete where you discuss your observations of his commitment (see Figure 2-1). Review the chart, if necessary: "It looks like your're operating around #6, John. Let's try to get to #8 tomorrow and #10 by match day. I know you have the ability, and I have confidence in you."

Finally, and most importantly: *You* must always demonstrate commitment in the 9–10 range. You should be the model the kids can imitate. Point out to them how the team has succeeded or improved because of their commitment.

It is hoped that in time your wrestlers will realize the benefits of being committed. You can foster their desire to become more committed through weekly discussions, personal notes, brief evening phone calls, or motivational letters from alumni.

*"Once a man has made a commitment, he puts
the greatest strength behind him . . .
Once a man has made this commitment,
nothing will stop him short of success."*

—(FROM VINCE LOMBARDI)

Our wrestlers need to learn the true meaning of commitment, and it is up to us, the coaches, to teach it to them. Their level of commitment will also rise if you let them share ownership of the team.

SHARING OWNERSHIP OF THE TEAM

Should coaches share control of their teams with the wrestlers? The idea itself seems contradictory, if not absurd. We all know that coaches, not athletes, should be the leaders. However, that's not always the case.

"People acting together as a group can accomplish things which no individual acting alone could ever hope to bring about."

—(FROM FRANKLIN D. ROOSEVELT)

When wrestlers have a sense of responsibility to themselves and their teammates, they tend to use it wisely and for the good of the team. At first, you may be uncomfortable sharing ownership with your team. You might equate it to turning the asylum over to the inmates, but with the right approach this can be an effective strategy. You see, we need to do more than tell wrestlers to be champions. We need to help them create the circmumstances in practice that make championships happen. Following are the methods and merits of teaching wrestlers to "own" their team.

When the team assembles on the first day of practice form a close circle and deal with three questions:

☑Why are you here?

☑What do you want to accomplish this season?

☑What is one personal item you can share with us?

This question-answer process takes about 20–40 minutes (depending on the size of your team) and usually involves some serious thought on their part (How often are athletes required to voice their goals to teammates?), especially by the younger guys who may not be certain yet what they want to accomplish. More importantly, everyone listens. As the returning lettermen speak, the newcomers learn why the sport is enjoyable and what is possible for them.

Answers vary for each question, of course, yet there is a common thread that connects all responses. Their answers to the first question often reflect their need to be part of a group. One study reveals that this need to socialize, called "affiliation," is the primary factor for athletes joining any particular team. Accordingly, kids seem to consider gaining friendship as a more important goal than achieving awards. Typical responses to the first question are, "Because my friend wrestles," "I don't like basketball and wrestling is perfect for guys like me," and "It looks like fun."

Teenagers, by nature, are often idealistic. This becomes quite evident when they respond to question #2. You may hear the following:

"Be champions of the conference."

"Get in great shape."

"Go undefeated."

"Win the State Tournament."

Obviously, they have high expectations for the team, and from this a *group* attitude toward team success emerges. They discover that many of them have the same goals; they all want to have a winning, competitive team. The coach here can infer also that they want practices to be intense, yet enjoyable. Through their own words, they have become unified toward a common purpose and outcome—challenging practices and a successful season.

For the final question, it may be as brief as "Where do you live?" or "What's your favorite movie?" or something more complex like "What's the craziest thing you've ever seen in this school?" or "How would you define courage?" Some good-natured teasing may occur, but humor helps ease the tension some of the wrestlers may feel about beginning a new season. Be sensitive, of course, to their socioeconomic and cultural backgrounds. For instance, questions about dating or parents could embarrass some kids.

Share control and responsibility. The head coach's input up to this point has been minimal. The athletes have done all the talking, even most of the decision making, especially regarding team goals. The coach has simply directed whose turn it is to speak next. A wrestler's intrinsic motivation improves when he senses being "in control." Conversely, if he has little or no control, he tends to be less motivated. Offer them control from day one; share responsibility with them.

Don't misunderstand. Coaches can't ignore their status as team leaders. They still must make many decisions in consultation with their coaching staff. However, the wrestlers can be involved in many issues regarding team objectives and direction, as in the following:

Scheduling:	"We have a choice of three tournaments next year. Which one would you like to compete in?"
Motivation:	"Guys, I'm not giving the pep talk today. You are. Johnny, tell Jimmy what he needs to do today to win."
Technique:	"Brian, show us how you hit your single leg so well. Begin with the set up and end with the finish."

Plan your practice, but don't be afraid to involve kids in that process as well. Once again, it involves giving the wrestlers choices:

"Should we do our sprints first or at the end?"

"What are the takedowns you think we need to work on now?"

"Lift weights or climb the ropes?"

Coaches can take this strategy a step further and give wrestlers a 10–15 minute time span each practice to work on mastering their weakest skills, a period where they can work together or alone on the techniques or skills they need to master. In short, they're "creating" the foundation for their own success. Typically, you'll notice groups of three or four choosing an activity (drilling double legs, for example) and then motivating each other until it's completed. It is not uncommon to observe seniors teaching freshmen or the talented kids encouraging the untalented.

The coaches can also give individual attention to each wrestler through the course of a week's practice. The only rule is that all wrestlers must stay active (running, drilling, jumping rope, lifting) during this session. This time is allotted for them to work on skills, not rest.

By the first competition, the intent is for the wrestlers to feel responsible for the team's success, to support each other, and *to own* the team. Furthermore, give time each practice (five minutes at the beginning or at the end) for them to discuss their expectations for that practice or the strategy for the next competition. Coaches can join the discussion but only as participants, not as leaders.

It can be awkward at first to give up control to your team. But as coaches, we need to do more than tell them to be champions. We need to help them create the circumstances in the practice room that make championships happen. There, wrestlers can be taught to define each week (possibly each day) what needs to be accomplished. At other times, coaches should discover what motivates each wrestler personally and then lead him to make solid commitments to both team and individual achievement.

The results of this approach can be rewarding. Once coaches learn to share responsibility and become partners with their wrestlers, the kids take more pride in team success and have more at stake in team achievement. This method of coaching places more trust in the wrestlers, which has a positive effect on their self-esteem. As an added benefit, you've taught them more than how to win a game; you've taught them how to win in life.

"We all came together six months before the 1980 Winter Olympics with different styles of hockey and different ethnic beliefs . . . but we made ourselves a team . . . Individually, we could not have done it."

— (FROM MIKE ERUZIONE, CENTER FOR THE 1980 USA OLYMPIC HOCKEY TEAM)

DEVELOPING YOUR COACHING STYLE

Coaching style is the summary of your personality when you enter the practice room or competition. It has little to do with what you wear and a lot to do with how you act and what you say. It is how your wrestlers know you and how they act when they're around you.

The wrestlers must respect your status as their coach. Establish your credibility, therefore, as quickly as possible. Credibility is probably most important at the beginning of the season to get wrestlers responding effectively to you. Raphael Taylor participates on the varsity football, wrestling, and track teams at Cleveland Heights High School and always checks to see if his coach "knows what's best, knows what he's doing, and knows how to go about it. I made it to States because my coach got to know me better than I know myself. He knew what I was capable of."

You can demonstrate your credibility in several ways:

☑Show an effective knowledge of wrestling skills;

☑Act in a friendly and understanding manner;

☑Be dynamic and enthusiastic;

☑Remain confident in every situation;

☑Treat all wrestlers in a fair and consistent manner; and

☑Have a history of positive team performances.

They must see you as someone competent enough to lead them, someone even willing to take risks to improve their individual performances. One veteran coach adopted a wrestling program at a high school that had rarely experienced any kind of success. His credibility came from "building a successful program at the school. I saw that I had to create an environment with a family approach. A coach has to be a leader. Demanding. Enthusiastic. A motivator. A coach in today's society must work *with* players, not be their dictator."

The wrestler needs to believe you care and that you know what you're talking about. Wrestlers can tell when a coach isn't being honest or consistent. Respect and understanding have to go both ways.

Tom Landry, former Dallas Cowboy head coach, was noted for his quiet, yet strong, coaching style. He explains that "leadership is a matter of having people look at you and gain confidence by seeing how you react. If you're in control, they're in control."

Your coaching style should be easily respected and admired. It should be based on dignity and diligence. But there are many coaching styles for coaches to adopt.

DEFINING COACH AS DIPLOMAT VS. COACH AS DICTATOR

The control any coach exerts on his team has a major influence on the team's success. The dictator's philosophy is straightforward: "It's my way or the highway." Here, the coach makes all the decisions. The wrestler's duty is to follow through immediately on the coach's demands. There are some serious faults to this approach. The wrestler may perform only for the praise of the coach or to avoid his anger.

Many coaches feel more comfortable with this role because they like being in control. And often the wrestlers are never uncertain what to expect or how to act in his presence. For these coaches I would ask: How much control is necessary? What defines control? Also:

—What rules are necessary?

—Why are they necessary?

—Who will devise the rules?

—What are the consequences when a rule is broken?

—How will the rules be checked?

—How will the rules be enforced?

Keep in mind when you devise your rules that the punishment you have should be based on the behavior, not on the individual involved. Regardless of major or minor violations, rules have to be handled fairly, consistently, and as soon after the infraction as possible.

Former NFL Coach Bud Grant says: "When making decisions, there are three things you have to watch out for. The first is that you can never be afraid of what the critics will think or say. The second is to not make decisions too soon. If you make them before you have to, you'll have a hard time changing your decision should new information become available to you. The third is that when your decision is to make a rule, you had better be prepared to enforce it. If you are not, then don't make the rule."

The coach who prefers the role of diplomat consults the wrestlers about rules and penalties. Here, the team establishes the conditions and consequences for group and individual behavior. You won't lose control or credibility by seeking their input; in fact, your wrestlers will respect you more for allowing them to share in the formation of the rules that govern the team.

There may even be differences between the rules you establish for practice and those you have for competitions. The punishment and reward system has to be carefully developed (with both the school's administration and wrestlers' parents in mind).

Experienced coaches are clear about the following:

- ☑ attendance and punctuality;
- ☑ how to care for uniforms and equipment;
- ☑ being cooperative with teammates and coaches;
- ☑ acceptable behavior at practice and during competition;
- ☑ treatment of locker room facilities (home and away);
- ☑ attentiveness to instructions; and
- ☑ use of alcohol, drugs, and tobacco.

Diplomatic coaches involve the wrestlers at the first team meeting or at the first practice in arranging the rules the team needs to follow in order to achieve the goals they establish. During the course of the season, coaches need to be prepared to deal with stealing, fighting, obscenity, lost equipment, and lack of effort. Positive reinforcement for following rules often works better than negative reinforcement when rules are violated. Coaches need to consider if they are more concerned with what wresters **should not** do vs. what they **should** do. These rules should be evaluated as the season progresses.

Whether you choose to be a dictator or a diplomat, you need to remain consistent and fair with your wrestlers.

MAKING WRESTLERS "COACHABLE"

When you begin to coach, you probably discover at least one athlete who wants to be on the team but doesn't want to be coached. They may like to compete, even enjoy working hard at practice, but they don't want any input from you. They are, in short, "uncoachable."

Frequently, coaches define "coachability" in terms of how well the athlete follows directions or acquires the skills they teach. A coach may expect "coachable" wrestlers to have a good rapport with him, to respect him and his decisions, and to involve him if they have personal problems.

Wrestlers are more likely to be coachable when they see their coach smile, when he knows all their names, and when he listens, praises, motivates, and encourages them. An effective coach expects responsibility, respect, and honesty. He comes prepared and shows commitment. If kids can see that, it's easier to make them coachable.

When problems occur, coaches sometimes doubt the wrestler's willingness to be coached. There are many signs that indicate whether the wrestler is uncoachable:

1. Does he refuse to train with the rest of the team?

2. Does he sulk, whine, or complain when things don't go his way?

3. How much does he blame others for his own failures?

4. Does he behave in a belligerent way or get in fights with teammates?

5. Does he constantly make excuses?

6. Does he often fail to try his or her best at practice or in competitions?

7. Does he perform poorly in school and defy teachers?

8. Does he "showboat" during competitions or berate opponents?

9. Does he refuse to adhere to any training schedule or fail to be punctual at meetings or practice?

10. Does that athlete demonstrate disrespect for you or constantly test your authority?

This type of wrestler may continually avoid the coach or make excessive demands of him (for example, in regards to special equipment or extra time). The uncoachable athlete may find fault with the way the coach manages the team and disrupt practice to argue aspects of technique or strategy. Instructions have to be repeated, equipment or uniforms have to replaced, and confrontations with teammates have to be arbitrated.

Such disruptive behaviors make everyone uncomfortable and tense. Dr. Bruce C. Ogilivie, Ph.D., and Dr. Thomas A. Tutko, Ph.D., researched athletes like this and published their results in *Problem Athletes and How to Handle Them*. They concluded that coachability is one of the most essential characteristics for superior athletic performances.

When confronted with such a wrestler, a common first reaction is simple: Get rid of him. But if you see the potential for change, then there is a technology for dealing with this type of individual. The key point is to determine the wrestler's level of trust. Maybe he has been exploited before and now finds it difficult to have any kind of an effective rapport with a coach. Can he see you as one he can easily trust?

Ironically, when the coach approaches the uncoachable athlete in a sincere attempt to communicate, the dialogue often backfires. For the coach, the conversation means advice and compassion. To the wrestler, it's criticism. What, then, should you do? Ogilivie and Tutko offer some guidelines:

1. Be reliable by saying what you will do and doing what you say.

2. Be careful about scheduling workouts—put them in writing and post them in the locker room. Then be punctual with your own attention to these activities.

3. React positively when wrestlers offer reasonable suggestions for change.

4. Give athletes options.

5. Don't make promises you can't keep.

6. Avoid being judgmental; show tolerance for their inadequacies.

7. Don't overemphasize their failures, especially as a means to change their inappropriate behavior.

8. Don't get into power struggles (or be manipulated).

9. Remind the wrestler of your position as coach; your obligation above anything else is to the team as a whole.

10. Negate any hostility with a calm and disarming demeanor.

11. Don't give the uncoachable athlete responsibility as a means of changing his behavior (like making him a team captain).

12. Don't lose patience.

13. Be cautious about using criticism.

14. Don't let his actions negate your ability to coach the rest of the team.

15. Don't be afraid to dismiss the wrestler from the team, regardless of his talent or potential.

It takes time and effort on the coach's part to deal with a difficult wrestler, and it may or may not turn out that it is time well spent. A veteran coach who has had winning teams at three different schools is always willing to work with these kind of wrestlers. "A coach has to remember," he says, "how high school really was. A coach must always be ready to communicate and be flexible. Patience is also important. Sometimes you have to sacrifice personal time or adjust your priorities on what is really important."

In their research, Ogilivie and Tutko discovered that these types of athletes often operate under a feeling of fear. The wise coach, therefore, should "develop a subtle technique for talking about fear and its effects upon performance . . . Coaches who expose their own personal fears as experiences in athletics pave the most sensitive roads to dealing with this emotion." This fear often surfaces in wrestlers who are experiencing some type of pressure or stress.

I have found that potential conflicts with a wrestler are lessened when I first get clear about his specific goals (What does he want to accomplish?) either through conversation or his first meeting questionnaire sheet (see Section 3). Next, in order to change his behavior I try to understand why he's behaving that way (his point of view). I may show sympathy and tolerance but not resignation. Once we have clarified each other's point of view I present options that are both non-threatening and different (they can't be the same ones he's heard from parents or teachers). We then make a decision together and follow through until he realizes he can gain more from ending the conflict than from continuing it.

LINKING SIGMUND FREUD AND THE WRESTLING COACH

How much is success on the mat due to the wrestler's physical skills? How much is due to his frame of mind? The coach is constantly addressing the players' frustrations, worries, confidence, and self-esteem. So how much of a psychologist or psycho-analyst does a coach have to be?

You don't have to be Sigmund Freud. You do, however, have to be prepared to define the emotional and psychological state of the individual wrestlers. In other words, what is their level of motivation? How fast do they learn? How do they react to success? To failure?

Clearly, you have to have faith in what you are coaching and you have to have faith in your kids. That means getting them to believe in themselves and you. You are not a babysitter; you're a professional, and your wrestlers need to recognize that.

Part of being a professional is to demonstrate your own self-confidence and patience, especially through those difficult periods (losses). Create a supportive atmosphere in the practice room and the locker room so that your wrestlers know you are concerned for their welfare and passionate about their success.

Build self-esteem. When you detect wrestlers with poor self-images, help them remove such negative beliefs the same way a person eliminates a bad habit. Remind them daily that they are competent, successful athletes to force that message into their unconscious belief system. Allow time in practice for kids to imagine themselves winning big matches or stepping onto the top spot of the victory platform. This can't be idle daydreaming but focused visualization. Finally, show kids in practice how they're getting better, how their training has turned their failures into successes, in order to re-affirm their positive self-images. This entire process may take time, maybe an entire season, but it is time well spent. Success on the mats will surely follow.

ACHIEVING STRESS MANAGEMENT—YOURS AND THEIRS

Coaches and wrestlers confront stress every day. So much stress, in fact, that many of them choose to avoid it by quitting. Some sports psychologists call this "burn out." Other terminology is "mental fatigue" and "getting stressed out." What can the coach do to turn worry into winning, and tension into triumph? Coaches need some lessons on the psychology of pressure and the power of positive thinking.

Feeling pressure is, in effect, a complaint about a problem. Whether the goal is to master a single leg takedown or escape in the third period, a wrestler may feel there's *something* wrong and he can't succeed. Suddenly, more than one obstacle exists: the actual problem and anxiety.

Most of us try to hide our anxiety, but this is the wrong way to go. Although unpleasant, all this worry must be talked about and brought out into the open. The pressure, even the feeling of fear, has to be acknowledged. The stress can't be ignored or belittled.

Both the coach and wrestler need to treat stress with patience. Understanding pressure means dealing with anxiety, especially the anxiety of an uncertain outcome. For too many wrestlers, their imaginations dramatize failure rather than success. Their opponents become stronger than they really are and their own weaknesses are magnified.

CONTROLLING THEIR EMOTIONS WITHOUT LOSING THEIR INTENSITY

Stress cannot be overcome with emotion. Disgust, anger, or rage do nothing to improve skills or smarts. Athletes and coaches should exert faith in their abilities, not fury. Roy Campanella achieved great success as a major league baseball player and coach. He also confronted his paralysis with the same dynamic attitude. He gives excellent advice: "When you're in a slump, you don't feel sorry for yourself. That's when you have to try harder. You have to have faith, hope, and conviction that you can lick it . . . You just have to be mentally tough."

For the wrestler, there are techniques to defeat stress:

☑Use a coach, fellow athlete, family member, clergyman, or teacher to help you talk out the problem.

☑Establish a means of relaxation that includes some form of meditation, deep breaths, and a warm-up that leaves you relaxed and alert.

☑Listen to all instructions carefully. This eliminates any uncertainties about what is expected or demanded of you (especially before a match).

☑Accept yourself as a strong, worthy competitor who can succeed.

"I made up my mind before I became a head coach that I wouldn't become a crybaby or a complainer. I would take the personnel they gave me to work with and I would take the hard knocks as they came along. It would just be a way to speed up my learning process. But I would neither cry nor complain."

—(FROM MONTE CLARK, FORMER NFL COACH)

In truth, virtually all athletes perceive competitions as threatening because there is always a possibility of defeat. It is the unexpected that prompts stress to occur for most wrestlers.

Ogilivie and Tutko identify various symptoms of stress in the athlete:

1. has jerky, awkward physical movements;

2. has tension in neck and shoulders;

3. experiences stomach cramps and loss of appetite;

4. loses concentration;

5. isolates himself and withdraws from others;

6. talks about the season being over; and

7. overreacts to even minor problems.

Many potentially successful performances are lost just prior to a match due to getting 'psyched out,' losing confidence, becoming unfocused, or experiencing something unexpected. The wise coach must prepare his wrestlers to prepare for and cope with all potentially debilitating events.

What are the stress situations that can get in the way of success? Personal frustrations in school, arguments with family or friends, previous failures at a competition, and unfamiliar settings (i.e., five thousand fans at the District Tournament vs. two hundred at a dual meet) are all typical stress-inducing situations.

To help wrestlers cope with pressure, there are various steps the coach can follow:

1. Make practices like real competition. (This prepares the athlete for the actual experience. For instance, some coaches play loud music to portray crowd noise.)

2. Allow time in practice to talk about pressure or "the big match." (Do this one on one, if preferred.)

3. Emphasize top physical conditioning.

4. Give the wrestler a day off or try to lessen his responsibilities.

5. Enable the wrestler to obtain professional counseling, if necessary.

Dr. Martin Stein, a professor of pediatrics at the University of California, San Diego School of Medicine, clarifies that "the experience of tension or stress is a normal aspect of development. It's a part of every child's life, from infancy to adolescence." Coaches shouldn't feel hesitant about "taking the first steps to discuss a problem with school staff—nurses, teachers, counselors, or support workers—and the child's family." Stein offers two more strategies: teach in creative ways and be ready to communicate. Have wrestlers concentrate on tasks, not outcomes.

A successful coach/wrestler relationship requires a balance of respect, confidence, and comfort. Coaches must create an atmosphere that promotes all-out effort and provides rewards. A wrestler must feel a sense of control that will allow him the chance to enjoy and excell at wrestling. The wrestling season is a journey, sometimes a long one, for the wrestler who undoubtedly will encounter obstacles and difficulties. We coaches, therefore, must be prepared to be his guide and his counselor.

FIGURE 2-1 WEEKLY PROGRESS REPORT

WEEKLY PROGRESS REPORT

NAME _____   DATE _____

WEIGHT CLASS _____   CLASS _____   RECORD _____

Below is your rating in each category measuring your level of commitment this past week with ten indicating a high mark and one indicating the lowest mark. It should be your goal to improve in each category each week.

CRITERIA	RATING	COACHES' COMMENTS
DEDICATION AND DETERMINATION	_____	
MENTAL ATTITUDE	_____	
STRENGTH WORK	_____	
PHYSICAL CONDITIONING	_____	
COOPERATION WITH OTHERS	_____	
COMPETITIVENESS	_____	
ENTHUSIASM AND MOTIVATION	_____	
FOCUS AND LEARNING	_____	

SECTION 3

Organizing Your Program

You've heard the old cliche: Failing to plan is planning to fail. And, in truth, the statement is especially appropriate to the coaching profession.

"No matter how naturally gifted an athlete or team may be, the coach without a plan for the development of those talents will usually fail to unlock their full potential."

  —(FROM GEOFF GOWAN, NATIONAL TRACK AND FIELD COACH FOR ENGLAND, PUERTO RICO, AND CANADA)

"When I hire a coach I look for someone who has a concern for students and good coaching skills, and I especially consider their organizational skills."

  —(FROM JUDY KIRMAN, PRINCIPAL, ROOSEVELT HIGH SCHOOL, KENT, OHIO)

Before beginning any activity that involves a group that is directed toward a certain goal(s), you need to get organized. An efficient way to organize your wrestling program is to consider breaking down the season into three parts: the pre-season, the regular season, and the post-season.

PRE-SEASON ACTIVITIES

Step #1—Identifying and Recruiting Potential Wrestlers

Emma Lazarus of New York is responsible for the poetic lines which appear on the base of the Statue of Liberty. The final lines state:

"Give me your tired, your poor,
Your huddled masses yearning to breathe free,
The wretched refuse of your teeming shore,
Send these, the homeless, tempest-tost to me,
I lift my lamp beside the golden door!"

That's what many wrestling coaches, especially those in schools with small enrollments, are willing to do to fill all the weight classes of their teams. Should coaches approach recruiting wrestlers this way, or should a more selective process be used?

Only you can answer these questions. Some coaches only want the best athletes—the most skilled, the most motivated, the most talented. Other coaches are more willing to work with any athlete. Your choice depends on what you want to accomplish with your team and the type of commitment you are willing to make to achieve your goals. Whatever your final decision, effective recruiting cannot be overlooked. Ultimately, your effort here has a major influence on the team's ability to compete.

Before the season begins the coach must begin a comprehensive recruiting process in order to prompt a large turnout of student/athletes for the squad. But those student/athletes are not going to join your program if you cannot provide a satisfactory answer for their question "Why would I want to be a part of your program?" Your reasons have to be good ones, and your delivery has to be enthusiastic.

Here are sixteen ways to begin recruiting:

1. Get a list of returning wrestlers from the athletic director and check their eligibility and past records (be sure to acquire a list of all middle school wrestlers, too).

2. Ask administrators and school faculty, especially the physical education teachers, for names of potential athletes and then send these athletes a letter introducing you and the program (see Figure 3-1).

3. Take these lists and introduce yourself to these athletes, invite them to join the team and ask if they know others who may be interested.

4. Write a personal (not a form) letter to these athletes where you again encourage the athlete's participation and explain how you feel he can contribute to the kind of program you want to have (see Figure 3-2).

5. Have senior wrestlers (possibly returning letter winners) talk to younger athletes to encourage them to join the program.

6. Put up posters in the hallways, on bulletin boards, in trophy cases, and in locker rooms to highlight the sport and the benefits of being on the team.

7. Make several public address announcements that are both creative and motivational (see Figure 3-3).

8. Get cheerleaders and statisticians to talk to potential athletes about participating.

9. Ask popular faculty members to make brief announcements to their classes (and individual students) about your program (how they look forward to watching the team compete that season).

10. Request other coaches to assist in getting their athletes into your program (let them know that wrestling develops an athlete's lateral movement, strength, and endurance).

11. Visit the physical education classes to identify potential wrestlers.

12. Use a highlight tape (or motivational tape) during the students' lunch time that promotes wrestling.

13. Make a follow-up phone call during the evening to discuss and confirm your interest in that athlete's participation.

14. Have prominent alumni call or write that athlete explaining how wrestling benefited them.

15. Have the school libraries (middle school and high school) order wrestling magazines like *Amateur Wrestling News* and *Wrestling USA*.

16. Send a letter to parents informing them about your program (see Figure 3-4).

This recruiting process can be frustrating and exhausting at times if some students' responses aren't favorable. But don't become discouraged. The more kids you talk to the better your chances for developing a competitive squad. These strategies may seem like a "hard sell" approach, but the intent isn't to overkill. The intent here is to reach the young person in a variety of ways until he is convinced that you're sincere about including him in the program.

There are other things you can do. To encourage more participation, develop a favorable schedule, effective publicity in the local media, and any special events (coordinated with your athletic director) that could appeal to additional athletes.

Kids can also recruit kids. You can involve wrestlers who have found the sport to be so rewarding and enjoyable that they are eager to talk to younger kids who may be uncertain. One varsity letter winner at Richmond Heights High School says, "I decided to participate in sports after one of my friends told me to come to practice. I found out that it kept me healthy, and I really enjoyed it." "My buddies told me about wrestling. I had never done it before," admits Eric Birch of Olmsted Falls High School, "but I enjoy all organized sports. I was ready to try something new."

As their coach, though, be sure that your older wrestlers say the right things. "I tell them that I wrestle because it's fun and exciting," says another varsity wrestler. "But you have to be ready to push yourself."

You can involve other people as well. Use individuals outside the school to assist you in developing your program.

Step #2—Networking in the Community

Here, alumni, siblings, and parents are important. They can make phone calls, write letters, or talk personally to potential wrestlers who may yet feel uncertain about participating on the team. You should establish a nucleus of support for your program from parents who understand and respect your coaching philosophy. "I'll nonrenew a coach if he or she has a communnication problem with parents, students, or administrators," warns Joe Webb, principal at Mentor High School. "A coach has to get all these people to believe in his program." Section 9 clarifies methods for gaining community support.

Step #3—Completing Administrative Duties

This phase begins with the coaching staff (dealt with more thoroughly in Section 5). Here, objectives the coaches expect the team to achieve and the methods for accomplishing those expectations must be addressed. Organizational duties include:

1. Arrange your daily practice schedule and calendar (see Figure 3-5).

2. Get directions from your school to all away matches (to distribute to parents later).

3. Seek 2-3 volunteer coaches, 2-3 managers, and 4-6 statisticians (see Figure 3-6).

4. Arrange for guest clinicians (an expert on leg riding, for example).

5. Inventory your uniforms and equipment (use your athletic department's Supplies Request Form to order necessary equipment like tape or headgears).

6. Arrange for scrimmages with other schools.

7. Arrange for matches to be videotaped by a parent or assistant coach.

8. Determine and design your Wrestler of the Week Awards (a t-shirt, certificate, trophy, etc.).

9. Order wrestling shoes for kids who request them (make a p.a. announcement for an entire week before sending in the order).

10. Consult with your athletic director about his/her expectations for the team and the use of the school facilities through the season.

Most of the team's specific expectations are officially determined after the first team meeting, but performing some pre-planning is crucial to future success. This not only gives a foundation but also a sense of direction for your program.

Step #4—Conditioning Sessions: Strength Training, Running, and Agility Drills

I like to begin pre-season conditioning six weeks before the season (approximately October 1), much like the armed forces use a six-week boot camp to train recruits. Some coaches like to begin in August when the football season starts, but I find the six-week period to be effective for three main reasons: (1) wrestlers don't become burned out; (2) it enables (if not encourages) the guys to participate in fall sports; and (3) I can coach a fall sport and spend more time at the multitude of administrative duties required in preparing the wrestling season.

Pre-season conditioning sessions are not just for getting the guys in shape. They should also be designed to encourage new athletes to gain confidence about participating in wrestling and enable you to establish a strong rapport with them.

A typical pre-season program is run three days a week—Monday, Wednesday, and Friday—for approximately one-and-a-half hours per session. Each session should duplicate, in part, the kind of practices you plan to conduct during the regular season. However, if your state athletic association prohibits coaches from teaching specific wrestling skills, you should not include any in your training sessions.

Begin every session on time with a brief meeting where you distribute and collect participation forms (physical cards, insurance waiver forms, etc.), explain the correct practice gear (either running shoes or wrestling shoes, sweatshirts or t-shirts), encourage the guys to recruit other athletes, and stress the importance of hustling through all drills.

Next, put the team through a detailed warm-up that gets them perspiring and prepared. Follow this with agility drills like the following:

☑Forward and backward rolls (tumbling)

☑Shuffle and carioca drills

☑Jumping rope and plyometrics

☑Spin drills and partner lifts

☑Aerobic exercises and step ups

☑Lower the level drills and balance (stance) drills

Training sessions must include weightlifting. Have each wrestler weightlift with a partner and chart the poundage on their lifts. There is a variety of approaches to weightlifting that you can adopt, so I suggest you utilize one that appeals to you and your kids collectively. You should also have them climb ropes and do chin ups, pushups, and situps as part of their lifting routine. See Figure 3-7 for a typical routine of pre-season agility drills.

Vary the running from sprints to distance running to bleacher steps to jogging. When doing distance running, begin with a simple mile run on the first day and work toward 5-6 miles by the sixth week. You may want to increase the distance if your athletes are completing the running segment in less time (see Figure 6-6 for more running activities). Conclude practice with a brief warm-down.

Keys are to keep these brief practice sessions fun and lively. You want the kids coming back and eager to improve. In this way you can set up the format and structure you want the team to follow during the regular season practices.

Step #5—Preparing for the First Team Meeting

A recent survey of nearly 3100 high schools across the country revealed that 82 percent of those schools' athletic groups held pre-season team meetings. Obviously, the tone and tempo of the season are revealed here. The coach has to be prepared for this very important meeting. The wrestlers will immediately discover your coaching style and personality. Your first impression is crucial.

Therefore, you need to be organized and enthusiastic at this first meeting. You must begin on time and quickly establish your credibility. The athletes should learn your background and your expectations. A brief, but detailed, introduction can accomplish this.

Distribute on paper or display on a chalk board the agenda of the meeting, and be sure that all distractions are eliminated. Introduce assistant coaches and any related personnel (trainers, managers) and clarify their responsibilities and authority.

What the wrestlers learn about the coach here is important, but the coach also needs to learn some things about them. Have them complete a personal data form and a brief questionnaire (see Figure 3-8).

A discussion about the team's goals and direction should follow. Deal with effort and eligibility, commitment and courage, rules and respect, sacrifice and success. Invite them to contribute ideas about team goals and practices. What are their expectations? What kind of activities have helped them win in the past? What kind of things haven't worked?

Establish that you are in partnership with them, that your primary goal is to empower them to compete successfully. Explain that you are committed to coaching them and that you expect them to be coachable. Be sure to conclude on a positive note and remind them of the date, time, and place of their first practice.

After the first team meeting, you and your coaching staff need to finalize all plans for the coming season. Be sure you have managers and statisticians arranged to assist the team, that team t-shirts are ordered, that all forms have been distributed and collected, and that transportation (bus) to away scrimmages and matches has been arranged.

As additional organizational and time management aids, some lists are included in the reproducible pages at the end of this section that you'll find helpful in announcing the first scrimmage (Figure 3-9), the first match (Figure 3-10), and sectional tournaments (Figure 3-11).

REGULAR SEASON ACTIVITIES

Strategy #1—Managing the Team and Finding Peer Leaders

"Without organization and leadership toward a realistic goal, there is no chance of realizing more than a small percentage of your potential."

—(FROM JOHN WOODEN)

Whether you coach a YMCA team or a Division I college program, the obligations and functions for proper team management are the same. Athletes require and deserve a structured and disciplined approach by the coach. Preparations and practices cannot be arranged haphazardly. Your wrestlers need to know what to expect and how to respond regarding the activities the coaching staff plans. In this way, the coach becomes the catalyst for the wrestler's potential.

Being a good coach requires the skill to "manipulate time," says a varsity coach with over 20 years of experience. "You have to have the ability to rapidly adjust practice and game plans that aren't working and paint for the kids a clear picture of what you want them to do. Coaching constantly challenges my creativity." For a coach-wrestler relationship to be successful, the wrestlers have to understand where your main focus is at all times. They need to know that your decisions are sound, and that there needs to be a progression from the basics to advanced techniques. Organization, discipline, and hard work are essential.

The time allotted for practice, your competition schedule, and the length of the season can determine the activities you plan for your wrestlers. Effective planning for practices is discussed in Section 6, but consider these important fundamentals:

1. Every practice needs to have specific objectives.

2. Athletes need to know clearly the reasons for accomplishing those objectives.

3. Practice should never be punishment.

4. Unless injured, all athletes should be participating all the time during practice.

5. Practice should be an enjoyable and challenging experience.

Effective team leaders are crucial to team management and success. They may not be the ones who lift the most weight on the benchpress or yell the loudest during drills but most often earn the most respect and show the most dependability. This wrestler arrives early for practice ready to learn and often stays afterwards to master a technique. He never complains and is excited about competing. Both the coach and the team can count on this guy.

An effective coach seeks out and works with the team leaders. You should give them meaningful responsibilities and include them in matters that involve disciplinary measures. Your better team leaders have a clear understanding of their responsibilities and goals. They like to see both themselves and their teammates improve. Allow them, in fact, opportunities to address teammates ("Captain's Talks") either before or after practices.

Other responsiblities for team leaders (captains) include:

1. lead the warm-up before practice and matches;

2. help maintain discipline in the locker room;

3. lead by example;

4. eliminate any hazing of younger wrestlers;

5. help determine strategy for next opponent;

6. recruit more athletes into wrestling;

7. decide the uniform to be worn (if you have several) for a competition; and

8. communicate effectively with both teammates and the coaching staff at all times.

The most effective captains, or leaders, are characterized by having a take-charge attitude and a high level of commitment. They want to be leaders! If you thrust leadership on any individual (maybe the kid who had the best record the previous season) the results can be disasterous. This action could cause him to experience too much pressure, and he may resent you for it. You might offer leadership status to an individual on a temporary basis and decide together afterwards if you both are satisfied. Just be sure to work cooperatively with your team leaders and avoid treating them as servants.

Finally, make sure your staff is prepared for the regular season and each coach knows his responsiblities. In this way, your plans for the season are ready to be completed successfully.

"Always have a plan and believe in it. I tell my coaches not to compromise. Nothing good happens by accident—it happens because of good organization. There must be a plan for everything and the plan will prevent you from overlooking little things. By having that plan, you'll be secure and self-doubts will never become a factor."

—(FROM CHUCK KNOX, NFL COACH)

Strategy #2—Utilizing Alumni—One Day at a Time

Former wrestlers, if given enough notice, often love to return to the school and teach younger athletes the techniques and tactics that helped them become successful. Utilize them. Their participation as instructors can enhance practices and lead to kids mastering especially difficult techniques.

Strategy #3—Developing 7-12 Program

The boys in your school should understand that wrestling accommodates all sizes and shapes. Even in some small schools, therefore, it is not uncommon to have between 50–150 total boys engaged on the middle school, freshmen, junior varsity, and varsity teams. They should also realize that wrestling teaches them to work hard, persevere through adversity, and sacrifice to reach a goal.

One way to introduce wrestling to younger athletes (grades 7–8) is in their physical education classes and through an intramural program. Encourage the teacher to put the boys through some basic drills and provide some videotapes for class use. During your free period try to put the class through a brief clinic. Before the season (and possibly during the post-season as well), organize wrestling intramurals after school and hold a tournament at the completion of the training sessions. Then invite all participants to join the middle school or freshmen team.

Top high school wrestling programs depend on an effective feeder program, which for most schools is the junior high team where young men are introduced to the excitement of the sport and learn the fundamentals. On the junior high/middle school team, athletes can gain the necessary experience on the mat in practice and in competitions, which prepares them to be successful high school wrestlers. These experiences are tremendous learning opportunities. Without them, it is rare for these younger wrestlers to achieve success at the high school level.

This is why serious attention must be given to the junior high/middle school squad. Here, the youth wrestler can step into a training regimen where he learns the fundamentals, develops an enthusiasm for the sport, and begins setting goals related to his success in both the junior high and high school programs.

These younger wrestlers need to know that although amateur wrestling is given less media attention compared to football, basketball, and baseball, there are still over 1.5 million wrestlers in the United States. Unlike football and baseball, it is also one of our major Olympic sports. Through USA Wrestling and the Junior Olympics, junior high wrestlers have the opportunity to engage in local, state, regional, and national competitions against opponents of similar ages and weights. In fact, few sports are organized as effectively for athletes across the country who wish to compete year round.

Encourage younger athletes to participate by posting signs in their physical education locker room and cafeteria. Have high school wrestlers converse with them about wrestling and work out with them occasionally in an intramural session or physical education class. Order wrestling magazines, and, if the equipment is available, put wrestling videotapes in the junior high library. You can also involve junior high girls by teaching them how to score a wrestling match and inviting them to make contributions to the junior high team by designing a program or working as managers.

For both the junior high and high school team, be sure you have proper facilities for practice, although there are several championship-caliber squads who practice on school stages or gym balconies. In fact, the first Kansas State—Air Force Academy match was held in the hallway of the AFA library. But it is not unfair to demand your own wrestling room that has padded walls and 1–2 complete mats. Seek the same facility for the junior high team, although this is economically impractical for most school systems.

You may choose to have the junior high team practice with the high school team to ensure that techniques are taught correctly to both groups, but I would discourage this. Each team needs to establish its own identity and practice format. If you invite a special clinician for a day, then certainly have both groups learn and practice together.

When scheduling matches for the junior high and high school programs be sure to wrestle at least two schools outside your conference schedule who equal your team's skill level. Then schedule two superior teams in order to expose your kids to the characteristics of good wrestling programs: their aggressive style of wrestling, their conditioning, and their fan support. To be sure, do not include more than two teams like this for either the junior high or high school schedule since you don't want to damage the confidence of your kids too easily. You can also arrange, after receiving permission from your administration, a competition that requires your team to travel a significant distance and stay overnight. Wrestlers enjoy the special status and experience of traveling to a distant school and staying in hotel rooms (or with host families) for a match or tournament. This would certainly be a highlight of their season.

Another key element to proper scheduling is to avoid any conflicts with your school's basketball teams or drama club. Set the starting times to promote large attendance by parents and students. Be sure that your junior high wrestlers can attend your high school matches for free and have your high school wrestlers attend in group at least one junior high match.

Encourage your administration to host one tournament—either junior high or high school—to expose (1) the student body to the excitement of the sport and (2) your kids to the excitement of individual awards. Your Booster Club can also use a weekend tournament to obtain revenues by selling food, beverages, and candy at a concession stand.

The head coach has to be prepared to organize all phases of his wrestling program and instruct all members. He must be attentive to the needs of both the seventh grader and the senior. He must be sure that everyone is headed in the same direction.

Strategy #4—The Winning Way to Wrestle-offs

For many coaches, wrestle-offs can be organizational nightmares; for the wrestlers, these challenges can be even worse. However, if you can follow the basic guidelines offered here, wrestle-offs can provide (1) an effective method to teach wrestling skills; (2) a fair system for determining a starting line-up; and (3) the competitive edge kids need to win their weekend match.

WHY HAVE WRESTLE-OFFS?

Being the starter is the key factor in keeping most athletes and their parents happy. Unlike football, basketball, and baseball, wrestling has always provided teenagers a fair opportunity to become a starter on the varsity squad. In almost all sports the coaching staff has to determine a first team (the starters) and a second/third team (the substitutes). If these teams are not determined objectively and fairly, you can set yourself up to be overwhelmed by dissidents on all sides. In wrestling, the wrestler's own strength and skill determine if he is worthy of being varsity, not the arbitrary decision of the coach.

The wrestler's success, therefore, becomes his responsibility and the wrestle-off directly engages him in accepting that responsibility. No coach decides who is better. No parent can argue the outcome. One varsity wrestler adds: "The coach has to give all wrestlers a chance. He has to take time out to understand the team and show confidence in each guy."

Regardless of who wins the wrestle-off, the coaching staff should recognize the achievements at some level for every athlete. You have to care about individuals and be consistent. A varsity competitor adds: "A few times when I wasn't having a good day, my coach talked to me and got me back on track. A good coach should be someone wrestlers can talk to."

WHEN SHOULD YOU HAVE WRESTLE-OFFS?

I advise beginning challenge matches directly after your second scrimmage of the season (or two weeks before the first match). By then, all wrestlers, including novices, have competed in drill sessions, practice matches, and scrimmage matches. They've faced difficult practices and confronted aggressive scrimmage opponents. By practice #10 they should be mentally ready to wrestle-off a teammate.

WHERE SHOULD YOU HAVE WRESTLE-OFFS?

Of course, wrestle-offs usually occur in the practice room. Consequently, expert planning is needed to deal with these questions: (1) What about the wrestlers not involved in wrestle-offs? (2) How can teammate interference (disruptive cheering or coaching) be avoided? and (3) How can the coaches both officiate the wrestle-offs and train the rest of the team?

Here, your stamina will surely be tested. Here are some suggestions in chronological order to assist you in transforming challenge matches into an organized and instructional event.

Seven days before wrestle-offs begin . . .

Arrange for the wrestle-offs to be videotaped. Kids, especially the non-winners, need to see their mistakes. This also shows the team that the coaches care as much about improving their techniques as they do about establishing the varsity team.

Contact a local official(s) to referee the wrestle-offs. They need to practice their skills, too, and their presence prepares the boys for actual competition procedures.

Five days before . . .

Inform all wrestlers to select a weight class, explain the rules related to wrestle-offs and any weight allowance (usually 4–6 pounds is fair), and answer all questions so as to leave no misunderstandings about what they should expect.

Three days before . . .

Confer personally with each wrestler about the weight class he has selected. Learn if he has any apprehensions (making the assigned weight or performing well, for example) and eliminate them. You can explain that if he loses, more opportunities exist to challenge again. Remind him, if he's an underclassman or freshman, that he can still compete on the junior varsity squad.

Two days before . . .

List the wrestle-offs on paper (usually blank tournament bracket sheets will do if your team has many numbers, with any returning varsity wrestler as the top seed) and also announce them to the team. Post this paper on the locker room bulletin board. Remind them about the weight allowance limit. Contact your officials to politely remind them of the date and time you expect them in your practice room.

The day before . . .

Get the blank videotape you plan to use for taping the wrestle-offs. At practice, clarify to your team that although the next day's wrestle-offs imply competition among individuals, team unity is essential.

On the day of wrestle-offs . . .

Have the guys warm-up together before sending any wrestler not involved in a wrestle-off out of the room to weightlift, do distance running, view an instructional video, and/or work out with the junior high team. Send 1–2 coaches with them. Challengers stay in the room with you, another coach, and the officials. Conduct as many matches simultaneously as you can reasonably handle on your mat space. Have an assistant coach or manager confer immediately with any non-winner if he desires to challenge for another weight class. At the end of practice, organize the next set of wrestle-offs.

On the second day of wrestle-offs . . .

Follow the same procedure as the first day, but vary the workout for the rest of the squad. Replace distance running with sprints, weightlifting with aerobics, and the video with a lecture about proper nutrition.

On the third–fourth day of wrestle-offs . . .

For most teams, the number of wrestle-offs has lessened, including the guys who have attempted to challenge at different weight classes, and the varsity line-up is nearly established. At this point engage the entire team in matches directly after the warm-up. Three or four of these may be wrestle-offs officiated by the coaching staff. Later in practice, spend thirty to forty-five minutes reviewing common mistakes (using the videotape) made during wrestle-offs and work to correct them.

On the day after wrestle-offs . . .

Now it's probably time for one of your toughest practices but precede it by having the boys voice their reactions to competing in wrestle-offs. Did it make them nervous? Were they in shape? What did they learn? This isn't a time for complaints, only improvement. They need to recognize the need for wrestle-offs to test them both mentally and physically prior to competing against other opponents in actual competitions.

A grueling practice can shake the doldrums out of the non-winners and get everyone focused on the first match. To prevent any misunderstandings, at the end of this practice announce the varsity, junior varsity, and freshmen line-ups. Be sure all boys know when the next round of wrestle-offs begins the following week.

OTHER IMPORTANT POINTS

1. If any varsity wrestler is unable to compete due to illness or injury, he is still considered to be the varsity starter upon his return although another wrestler competed in his place.

2. If a varsity position is vacated, that weight class is declared "OPEN" and any wrestler can challenge for it. Only one victory over each competitor is required to earn that position. Example: when a varsity wrestler switches to another weight class.

3. If a varsity wrestler is challenged again he must be defeated twice in a row.

4. If strategy or injury dictates changing the line up after wrestle-offs have concluded, the coaches can determine the competitors per weight class for a dual meet after a pre-meet conference with the team.

In conclusion, communicate openly and effectively with the entire team. Be sure they understand your expectations and policies regarding wrestle-offs. And be consistent each week. Use these challenge matches as a means to make your team more competitive in practice and more intelligent about strategies. Be cautious of your approach when pointing out athletes' mistakes and lessen the emphasis you place on having a first, second, and third team.

Strategy #5—Involving Your Faculty and Administration

The key here again is communication. Keep your athletic director, principal, and superintendent informed about your plans. Consider your position as a team player in the school. You have to realize that many administrators are themselves burdened by the difficulties of supervising hundreds of other teachers and students combined. Therefore, they may not be able to offer much assistance.

They may also bury you in paperwork. Moreover, failing to keep up with this paperwork has ruined many young coaches. Dick Bliss, an athletic director for over 16 years at Aurora High School in Ohio, has often been disappointed by the coaches who "lack the willingness to pay attention to details and follow through with the administrative paperwork and equipment responsibilities at the end of the season."

What kind of paperwork should a coach expect? Before coaches even blow their whistles for the first practice at 99 percent of the schools across this country, they must distribute, recollect, and file a full cabinet of forms. These include:

1. an athletic department rules and regulations form which usually needs to be co-signed by parents;

2. an emergency medical authorization form;

3. an insurance waiver;

4. a physical examination card;

5. an equipment inventory sheet;

6. a personal information form; and

7. a gym lock and a locker card.

For Richard Corbin, an administrator at Griswold Senior High School in Connecticut, a coach's evaluation depends on his ability to handle this kind of paperwork. "The four key components I look for in a coach," says Corbin, "are his strength as a motivator, an innovator, a communicator, and an organizer. We want to know whether a coach hands in his paper work on time, meets deadlines, and runs an efficient practice."

Bill McGrain has earned many Southwestern Conference and Sectional Tournament championships as a head wrestling coach, but the achievement he values most has been "earning the confidence in the school district of my administrators and parents. They let me do my job, but it took many years to get to that. Of course, a coach always has to consider school politics and who you know."

Keep administrators informed about all events related to your wrestling program, both good and bad. Invite them to speak to the team at practices, possibly before a match. If they're unfamiliar with wrestling, teach them the strategies and the scoring. Help them understand the excitement and benefits of wrestling.

Administrators are also concerned about liability, another hot topic for today's coaches.

COACHES IN THE COURTROOM

Although today's coaches are used to gatorade showers, it was common many years ago for athletes to dump their victorious coaches in the locker room showers. That trend has certainly changed as too often the only place coaches are being dumped now is in a courtroom.

Robert Kanaby, the director of the National Federation of State High School Associations, worries about "litigation costs and frivolous lawsuits, which have unfortunately become a way of life." After 28 years of coaching wrestling at Fairfield High School in Ohio, Ron Massanek understands the consequences of being a coach: "Everytime we go to practice or a competition, we live with the threat of being sued." Clearly, more and more parents are initiating litigation against coaches.

Legal Point #1—What Makes You Negligent?

In one example, a New York City football player sued for over one million dollars when he was compelled to play in a game against a more competitive team in the Public School's Athletic League. After he was injured, his parents brought a negligence case against the coach and school. He won his case.

In Kansas, when the Smoky Valley High School football team finished a night time practice on August 23, 1985, Jeffrey Nichols followed his coach's instructions and ran to the locker room. In the darkness, Nichols could not see the grassy swale that provided drainage for the nearby playground. He stumbled, caught his balance, and staggered into the locker room. After experiencing back pain for one month, he sued. His suit declared negligence by the head coach for making players run in the dark. The coach won the case, but Nichols' parents have appealed.

These examples, although related to football, point out that coaches can be sued at any time. However, preventive measures that establish safety as a priority can lessen your chance of being found negligent. In many typical lawsuits the coach is joined by the school board, superintendent, and principal as defendants, but the coach is still the one who would be cited as responsible for any negligent act.

In determining any act of negligence by a coach the court first compares his actions to the behavior of a "reasonable" wrestling coach. The court then evaluates the defendant coach to see if he possesses the qualifications and skills normally found in all other coaches. In short, negligence can be found if the coach performs in any manner outside the normal standard followed by a prudent coach.

If the subjectivity here doesn't disturb you, it should. You can lessen your risk of liability by conducting practice with the wrestlers' health and safety in mind, taking precautions when you travel, and behaving professionally during all competitions. Negligence occurs most often for coaches who fail to either act cautiously or to foresee, as any prudent coach should, circumstances that could expose their wrestlers to injury or harm.

Legal Point #2—What Makes You Liable?

One jury decided a coach was liable after he "failed to provide . . . proper supervision, instruction, and equipment and that such negligence was legal cause for the student's injuries." In Louisiana, a wrist injury prompted a Francis T. Nicholls High School athlete to sue his coach, who had delayed in referring the boy to medical treatment. Here, the Louisiana Fourth Circuit Court of Appeals ruled that the coach was one third responsible in that he and the trainer had "breached their duty to refer the student for appropriate medical care."

Some parents have even filed lawsuits against youth coaches when they have not given their children enough playing time, an act that parents say stunted their kids' development towards earning college scholarships. Clearly, the domain of a coach's liability is quite large.

Coaches become immediately liable, according to most courts, when they place their wrestlers in situations that expose them to unnecessary risks, injuries, or harm. In basic terms, a coach is liable if he:

1. he fails to adhere to his coaching contract;

2. he fails to act according to the characteristics of a prudent person;

3. he neglects by ommission or causes by commission a wrestler's injury—e.g., not treating the injury immediately (ommission) or moving the injured wrestler unnecessarily (commission); and

4. his conduct results in any wrestler's physical loss.

Coaches can protect themselves and reduce the potential for a lawsuit if they do the following:

1. show the accident was unavoidable;

2. show the wrestler contributed to his own injury;

3. show the wrestler assumed the risks;

4. prove the accident was an act of God;

5. befriend athletes and parents and establish strong channels of communication;

6. distribute in writing sound policies and procedures, especially regarding emergency medical situations;

7. attend (along with assistant coaches) sports medicine clinics once or twice a year;

8. demand all wrestlers (and their parents) sign a "release" or "insurance waiver" form stating that coaches and school personnel are not liable for injuries (although these forms, in actuality, have little legal value);

9. offer wrestlers the opportunity to purchase supplemental health insurance;

10. travel only if all team members are covered by insurance (or have turned in an insurance waiver form);

11. supervise wrestlers at all times;

12. instruct their wrestlers effectively and thoroughly in the proper techniques that are recognized as appropriate by experts in our sport;

13. provide the proper equipment and document regularly your safety and maintenance checks of this equipment according to the manufacterers' specification;

14. replace all damaged or worn uniforms and equipment;

15. teach wrestlers and parents about the protective limitations of all equipment;

16. have a trainer and/or physician monitor all practices and competitions;

17. plan conditioning programs that prepare wrestlers effectively for competitions and evaluate all wrestlers' strengths and weaknesses prior to a competition;

18. have easy access to emergency medical personnel—that is, you have an accessibile telephone;

19. have first aid equipment readily available;

20. give immediate attention to any injury and use extreme caution before permitting an injured wrestler to practice/compete again;

21. prohibit boys from competing who are not physically or mentally prepared for the intense exertions required in wrestling;

22. document any wrestler's rules violations and explain the consequences of these violations to the wrestler and his parents;

23. demand wrestlers follow the instructions of any official;

24. maintain precise and complete written records, including notices of equipment defects, health and injury records (even minor ones), and memorandums to administrators; and

25. obtain as many statements as possible from witnesses of any accident or injury.

As long as we have sport, coaches could face the possibility of litigation. They just need to be better prepared. Along with the rule book, important reading might be a law manual. Ironically, in almost all lawsuits, plaintiff attorneys use other coaches as expert witnesses against the defendant coach. Moreover, athletes' parents can bring litigation against a coach up to two years after any incident. Careful planning and clear communication are the keys.

Legal Point #3—Insurance Waiver Forms

Use these (obtain copies from your athletic director) to protect yourself, the athletic department, and your school board from any insurance claims due to injuries. Wrestling is obviously a contact sport and a wrestler assumes the risk of injury when he chooses to participate. He (or his parents) is responsible, therefore, for his own insurance coverage once his parents sign this form.

Legal Point #4—Read the Rule Book

When planning practice activities or preparing for competition, great attention must be paid to the rules listed in the federation and your state rule books. Key items are to learn and then explain illegal holds and maneuvers, to document daily weight checks on a weight chart, to perform proper (and safe) techniques in practice, and to deal with any injuries carefully. These are the characteristics of a prudent coach.

THE POST SEASON

Some coaches close up shop at the end of the final competition and don't open it up until the first day of practice next year. Others schedule "open mat," weightlifting sessions, traveling teams, and conditioning workouts throughout the off-season. Obviously, both approaches have their faults and merits. Your approach will certainly depend on your coaching philosophy and the amount of time available to you in the post-season (possibly you're coaching a second or third sport).

The post-season is also a typical time to hand out awards to the athletes.

Step #1—Your Awards Program

Arranging an end-of-year awards program should take place at least one month in advance (Consult with your athletic director about your specific responsibilities here). Decide the type of awards you want to give out to your top wrestlers, who will be receiving those awards, and the criteria that accompany each award (see Figure 3-12).

Print this information in the pamphlet that is distributed to the parents and wrestlers at the awards program. Don't be afraid to share the wealth. In other words, try to honor as many different wrestlers as possible. It is also wise to allow the wrestlers to select (by private vote) the winner of an award.

Typical awards could be Most Improved (either from previous season to current season or from the beginning of the current season to its end), Coach's Award (the hardest working and most coachable athlete), Scholar-Athlete Award (given to the most accomplished student, either by GPA or academic honors, on the team), and Most Outstanding Wrestler. You might choose to distribute t-shirts that declare any championships won by the team or trophies for wrestlers who gained the most pins or tournament titles.

Use the awards program to acknowledge and thank all assistant coaches (including junior high or middle school coaches), the principal, assistant principal, athletic director, and trainers. Express gratitude to the school's booster club and other support groups (mention mothers and fathers by name), your statisticians, and any other table personnel. Announce any tournament winners and all-conference, all-district, or all-state selections; reward the varsity letter winners; and finally hand out your major awards.

Since parents are in attendance, use the time again to explain your expectations of the wrestlers in the off-season. You may want them to attend a summer camp, participate in conditioning sessions, compete in other school sports, or simply return some equipment or uniforms. Speak about their academics and their goals, the progress the team accomplished and the improvements that still need to come, the satisfaction you've had coaching, and the concerns you have for the following season. Possibly, play a promotional videotape or hand out pictures taken of the wrestlers during the season by a school photographer. As in your first team meeting with the athletes, end on a positive note.

Step #2—Review and Analysis of the Season

For Bill McGrain, the post-season is a time for detailed planning. "I begin by looking ahead at least three years to see what the program needs." He also reviews losses and "pays attention to the details in order to prepare for difficult times next year. I enjoy wrestling and want to stay with it even in the off-season. I want to lead by example." Evaluate the major weaknesses of your returning high school wrestlers (poor takedown skills, for example) and the number of middle school wrestlers you expect to participate on the high school team. Determine, if necessary, weight classes that might be without a participant so that you can begin a focused recruiting strategy.

Step #3—Personal Conferences—A Dialogue for Direction

Talking to wrestlers in the lunchroom, inviting them to workouts, meeting with your assistant coaches and evaluating the season, assisting seniors with college plans (possible scholarships)—these are just a few of the tasks a diligent coach should perform after his season has concluded. After speaking to returning wrestlers, follow up with an official letter detailing your expectations and plans (see Figure 3-13). See also Figure 3-14 for a reproducible form to give your wrestlers to evaluate the season.

Another important conference should be with the athletic director. Here, you can assess the season, order any replacement equipment, evaluate the assistant coaches, and review the needs of the entire program. Expect, of course, to hear some constructive criticism. Just as you continually seek improvement from your wrestlers, your athletic director should expect the same from you.

Step #4—Strength Training

Set up a weightlifting/rope climbing schedule or workout that your wrestlers can easily follow 2–4 times a week. You should encourage them to stay in reasonable shape by running (on their own). Assess their strength at their first workout and then test them at various intervals—four weeks, eight weeks, sixteen weeks. Again, since a variety of weightlifting programs exists, you should select the one that you and the wrestlers prefer together. Figure 3-15 at the end of this chapter gives a list of weight lifting exercises for specific parts of the body.

Step #5—Off-Season Wrestling Tournaments

In Ohio, such tournaments are in operation almost every weekend through April after the regular season has concluded. This is probably duplicated in many states. Coaches should allow the wrestlers and their parents to decide the tournaments where they wish to compete. Be ready to provide forms, directions, and information about these tournaments to the guys and their parents. You should also attend as many as possible to show your support and interest.

Encourage your wrestlers to participate in USA Wrestling, which offers tournaments and meets in every state for athletes of all ages. Their brochure declares their number one goal: "To offer competitions and educational programs for young athletes." Their events, scheduled annually, enable wrestlers to compete in the off-season and to improve their skills. The USA Wrestling Tournaments take place in the spring and summer on the local, state, regional, and national level.

You could also host your own open tournament where parents work the scoreboards and assistant coaches function as officials. Again, your booster club can operate a concession stand, and graduating wrestlers can help your mat statisticians score the matches. One local school hosts their "Mighty Mite" tournament in order "to bring wrestlers, coaches, fans, and parents together in a positive money maker."

As a head wrestling coach in your community you could form your own wrestling club and set up competitions with other clubs. You could travel across your state to train, compete, and socialize with other wrestling clubs. Don't transform the spring or summer months into a brand new season, but only expose those athletes who want to enhance their skills to experiences that can build their confidence and satisfy their competitive urges.

Step #6—Summer Wrestling Camps

Provide information to all wrestlers in grades 7–11 about their options for summer wrestling camps. Whether wrestlers attend a commuter camp or camp out of state, they can pick up valuable instruction on techniques and training that can increase their chances for success during the regular season. It's recommended you attend the camp with them as long as no personal obligations interfere. Once again, this demonstrates your support and interest and enables you to observe firsthand the techniques the camp clinicians teach your wrestlers.

Step #7—Team Retreat or Picnic

Team unity and friendship are developed through this activity. You can arrange this for any season of the year, depending on your personal schedule and goals. In the summer some coaches take their teams camping and canoeing while others have a picnic and softball game. One coach invited the entire team to his home during the season for a sleep over that involved video games, pool, ping-pong, pizza, and cards. Clearly, a strong sense of fellowship is established within the team, and the kids and the coaches strengthen their rapport. When arranging this activity be sure parents are clearly informed about all plans.

Step #8—Seniors and Scholarships

In truth, there are not enough college scholarships available for deserving high school wrestlers, even the champions, yet there are steps you can take to assist any talented senior on your team in getting the attention of a college coach. One way is a letter (see Figure 3-16) and resume (see Figure 3-17) that should be mailed during the midpoint of the season. This enables the college coach to monitor your wrestler for the remainder of the season. Follow up with a brief letter or phone call at the end of the season to learn if the college coach is indeed interested in your senior wrestler. Keep a file of letters written by college coaches who express an interest in any of your senior wrestlers.

There remain many duties the helpful coach should accomplish in the months that follow the end of his season. Keep in mind that the work is ongoing. Jim Vreeland, a coach and official for over 24 years at three different Ohio high schools, realizes that coaching doesn't end when the athlete graduates. "My success as a coach is not truly recognized until my athletes are years out of high school. My job is to use athletics to help build stronger, better people, ready to take their place in the world . . . There's a personal satisfaction and an inner fulfillment in helping young people grow."

FIGURE 3-1 LETTER OF INTRODUCTION TO POTENTIAL WRESTLERS

Dear John:

This letter is about the sport of wrestling:

—the oldest sport known to man, originating over 5000 years ago (baseball didn't begin until 1839, and basketball wasn't invented until 1891);

—a sport that has had as competitors some of the greatest men in history like Benjamin Franklin, Abraham Lincoln, George Patton (WWII General), and Norman Schwarzkopf (the commanding general of the Persian Gulf forces);

—a sport designed to permit any person of any size and weight to compete for goals and glory;

—a sport where success is determined not by the size of the team but by the size of your own heart!

And this letter is about you. If you're interested in joining the high school wrestling team, you are committing yourself to one of the greatest challenges of your life. And if you're willing to work hard, it can also be one of the most rewarding experiences of your life.

Our school has a tradition of wrestling excellence—just examine the trophies in the display case and the pictures of the state champions. We want you to be a part of that tradition. The greatest thing about wrestling is that you can succeed regardless of your size, speed, height, or weight.

You will have to think and act like a winner. That's the kind of attitude you need for wrestling.

Here are the important details:

Pre-Season conditioning: Begins Mon., Oct. 1, 2:45-4:15
                         Meet in the high school gym

First official practice: Monday, November 14
                         2:45-5:15 P.M. in wrestling room

I look forward to seeing you at conditioning.

Sincerely,

FIGURE 3-2 PERSONAL NOTE TO ATHLETES

Dear John:

Watching you on the football field this fall convinces me you have the skills and the stamina to be a successful wrestler. I would bet that your hard-hitting style of play at linebacker is a key reason our team's defense is so highly ranked in the conference. I think your abilities can only get better if you compete on the wrestling team this season.

Sure, it might be tough at first, but if you're not afraid of challenges and like one-on-one competition where you don't have to depend on an entire team to make the "big play," then wrestling is the sport for you. Talk to some of the guys who are on the team and ask them about it. I'm certain they'd like to see you join.

I want to see you on the mats this winter, but for now keep up the good work on the football field. Good luck in your game against _____ High School. Be a leader!

Sincerely,

FIGURE 3-3 P.A. ANNOUNCEMENT

Wrestling—It's not just a job, it's an adventure. Just ask the guys who won state titles for our school. In fact, the first boy who can identify the names of our school's first state champion and our **last** state champion will win a t-shirt.

Give the correct names to Coach _____ in Room _____ any time during the day. Keep in mind that wrestling practice begins in four weeks. It's a sport for any boy of any size, and that means you!

©1996 by Parker Publishing Company

FIGURE 3-4 LETTER TO PARENTS

CONGRATULATIONS!

Your son has made an important commitment regarding his decision to join the high school wrestling team. The coaching staff is very pleased to have your son as a member of the program, and we have organized our efforts to promote his individual success. Wrestling is a very demanding sport. It will require much effort and dedication from your son. We admire and respect him already for making this type of commitment.

OUR SEASON

The season officially begins on Monday, November 14 and continues through February. This means, of course, we will have practices each school day and on Saturdays. Practices run from 2:45 P.M. to 5:15 P.M. (showers follow). Our competitions begin in December (I have enclosed a copy of our schedule).

PRE-SEASON INFORMATION

I expect the boys not involved in a fall sport to engage themselves in a conditioning program at the school every Monday, Wednesday, and Friday after school from 2:45 to 4:15 P.M. They will weightlift, do agility drills, and run.

FORMS

Participation in wrestling also involves some important forms for both the wrestler and his parents to complete. I have enclosed them in this envelope. Please have your son return them to me as soon as possible.

THANK YOU

The coaches certainly appreciate your support in encouraging your son to wrestle. He's taking on a big challenge, and we know that he could experience some difficulties during the season. But if we work together, your son's wrestling season can be very rewarding for him.

We also look forward to seeing you at our matches. Parents can also order sweaters that display our school colors and name. An order form is enclosed.

Sincerely,

FIGURE 3-5 PRACTICE/MATCH CALENDAR

January 1995

Sunday	Monday	Tuesday	Wednesday	Thursday	Friday	Saturday
1	PRACTICE 2:45 - 5:15 PM **2**	PRACTICE 2:45 - 5:15 PM **3**	PRACTICE 2:45 - 5:15 PM **4**	PRACTICE 2:45 - 5:15 PM **5**	PRACTICE 2:45 - 5:00 PM GO TO BOYS BASKETBALL GAME 7:30 PM **6**	MATCH VS. _____ HS 7:00 PM BUS LEAVES 5:00 PM **7**
8	PRACTICE 2:45 - 5:15 PM **9**	PRACTICE 2:45 - 5:15 PM **10**	PRACTICE 2:45 - 5:15 PM **11**	PRACTICE 2:45 - 5:15 PM **12**	_____ HS TOURNAMENT 4:00 PM - WEIGH-INS 2:00-3:30 **13**	_____ HS TOURNAMENT WEIGH-INS 10-11:30 SEMIFINALS AT NOON **14**
15	PRACTICE 2:45 - 5:15 PM **16**	PRACTICE 2:45 - 5:15 PM **17**	PRACTICE 2:45 - 5:15 PM STUDY FOR FINAL EXAMS **18**	PRACTICE 2:45 - 5:15 PM STUDY FOR FINAL EXAMS **19**	PRACTICE 2:45 - 5:00 PM **20**	MATCH VS. _____ HS 7:00 PM BUS LEAVES 5:00 PM **21**
22	PRACTICE 2:45 - 5:15 PM **23**	PRACTICE 2:45 - 5:15 PM **24**	PRACTICE 2:45 - 5:15 PM **25**	PRACTICE 2:45 - 5:15 PM **26**	PRACTICE 2:45 - 5:00 PM SUPPORT BOYS BASKETBALL TEAM **27**	MATCH VS. _____ HS 7:00 PM ARRIVE AT SCHOOL 5:30 PM **28**
29	PRACTICE 2:45 - 5:15 PM **30**	PRACTICE 2:45 - 4:15 PM GO TO JUNIOR HIGH MATCH 4:30 PM **31**				

FIGURE 3-6 LETTER TO MANAGERS/STATISTICIANS

Dear _____:

Much thanks for volunteering to join our Mat Stats. Your participation is greatly needed and greatly appreciated. It looks like we're going to have an exciting and successful season, and we're glad you're going to be part of it. Here is what you will be expected to do:

1. attend all training sessions during Per. ___ to learn scoring;

2. work all sessions of our tournament and at our dual meets;

3. master the wrestling scoring system;

4. attend one after school training session to score a wrestle-off;

5. stay in contact with your advisor during each week of the wrestling season;

6. promote our wrestling team and sell ads for our wrestling program; and

7. attend the awards banquet at end of season.

The first meeting will be in Room _____ on _____ at 3:00 P.M. We look forward to seeing you there.

Thanks,

FIGURE 3-7 PRE-SEASON AGILITY DRILLS

Individual Exercises

1. Plyometrics:

Wrestlers leap or jump from spot to spot across a mat, maintaining bent legs and continuous motion. See Photo 3-1 for starting position.

PHOTO 3-1

2. Stance and Balance:

Wrestlers bounce on the balls of their feet, settling themselves quickly into a square or staggered stance when the coach blows the whistle. The next whistle starts them bouncing again. See Photo 3-2.

PHOTO 3-2

©1996 by Parker Publishing Company

FIGURE 3-7 CONTINUED

3. Tuck Jumps:

From a standing position, wrestlers begin jumping, bringing their knees to their chests each time and keeping their backs straight. Perform this drill in durations of 15, 30, 45, or 60 seconds.

4. Step Ups:

On a low bench or gym bleachers, wrestlers alternate the left and right foot stepping up rapidly without rest onto the bench until stopped by the coach's whistle. Perform this drill in durations of 15, 30, 45, 60, or 90 seconds.

5. Aerobics:

Here, continuous movement is required as wrestlers step or lunge in all directions as directed by a coach or a workout video. Perform this drill in durations of 15, 30, 45, 60, or 90 seconds.

Partner Exercises

1. Spin Drills:

With Partner A in base position, Partner B places his chest on A's back and his hands on A's head and hip (see Photo 3-3). At the whistle, B spins in one direction, changing direction each time he hears the coach's whistle. He must move in short, choppy steps while maintaining chest pressure on A's back, and push on A's head and arms through every rotation (see Photos 3-4 and 3-5). End the drill with a double whistle and have wrestlers switch positions. Conduct the drill in durations of 15, 30, 45, 60, or 90 seconds for each wrestler.

©1996 by Parker Publishing Company

PHOTO 3-3

FIGURE 3-7 CONTINUED

PHOTO 3-4

PHOTO 3-5

2. Partner Carries:

With Partner A on his back, B runs along the gym or mat's perimeter. At the whistle, wrestlers change their positions. Conduct this drill in durations of 30, 60, 90, or 120 seconds.

3. Wheelbarrow Runs:

Partner A carries above the knees the legs of B who faces the mat in a push-up position. On the whistle, A begins jogging, forcing B to move his arms stride for stride. This helps improve shoulder and arm strength while increasing overall endurance. A and B change positions at the whistle. Conduct this drill in durations of 30, 60, 90, or 120 seconds.

©1996 by Parker Publishing Company

FIGURE 3-7 CONTINUED

4. Partner Lifts:

Partner A wraps his arms around B in a bear hug manner, either trapping one arm, both arms, or neither arm. A them pops his hips in, lifts B, and walks 4–5 steps forward. Repeat this drill 4–5 times before changing places.

5. Hop Overs:

Partner A places himself in a prone, semi-push-up, and then base position, as B hops from side to side in rapid succession. Wrestlers change positions at the whistle. Conduct this drill in durations of 30, 60, or 90 seconds (see Photos 3-6 and 3-7.)

PHOTO 3-6

PHOTO 3-7

FIGURE 3-7 CONTINUED

6. Hip Heists:

Partner A maintains a base position as B positions his back square on A's head and shoulders (see Photo 3-8). On the whistle, B twists his hips and slides either leg beneath the other—hip heisting (see Photo 3-9). B should finish in control of A's head and arm as if sprawling (see Photo 3-10).

PHOTO 3-8

PHOTO 3-9

©1996 by Parker Publishing Company

FIGURE 3-7 CONTINUED

PHOTO 3-10

FIGURE 3-8 FIRST MEETING QUESTIONNAIRE

Name _____ Grade _____ Homeroom _____

Address _____

Phone _____ Birthdate _____

Current GPA _____ Other sports _____

<u>Wrestling Survey Questions</u>

1. What has been your greatest commitment to date?

2. What will make wrestling fun for you?

3. What could be a great achievement for you this year?

4. What are your personal goals this year?

5. What are you willing to do to accomplish your goals?

6. What are you willing to do to help the team be successful?

FIGURE 3-9 FIRST SCRIMMAGE ANNOUNCEMENTS

Each coaching staff's expectations for a first scrimmage may vary, but there are some general guidelines that all teams follow. Here are some basic comments coaches should make to their wrestlers to clarify their approach and attitude about a scrimmage situation to prevent any confusion or misunderstandings.

1. How coaches view the scrimmage situation

2. Coaches' expectations of wrestlers—following directions, using techniques taught in practice, being coachable

   Don't worry about mistakes—there is still much technique to learn

3. What to wear—shorts and blue t-shirt

4. Don't get pinned—come off your back in a hurry

5. Nutrition

6. Following training rules over the weekend—NO one last party

7. Scrimmage will be videotaped—we will view it during the following practice

8. Behavior on bus

9. Keep track of your equipment—your headgear and kneepads—it is very easy to get it lost with all the teams there

10. Captains will lead warm-up

FIGURE 3-10 FIRST MATCH ANNOUNCEMENTS

Wrestlers never doubt their coaches expect them to try to win their matches, but they may be unclear about the agenda or format of the dual meet. Younger wrestlers especially often have little familiarity with the organization of this competition. Coaches, therefore, should provide the following general directions prior to the match.

1. Check your alignment with the official.

2. Make your weight—the scale and the coaches have no sympathy for you.

3. Hair, fingernails, and facial hair must be dealt with beforehand.

4. Coin toss—captains—who goes out on the mat first.

5. Captains rule locker room.

6. Behavior in and outside the locker room—on the team bench—how you represent us, the school, and yourself—do not leave the team bench (sit and support your teammates) unless given permission by a coach.

   NO unruly behavior, especially toward an official or opposing fans.

7. Wearing your warm-ups—when can you take them off?

8. Any uniform problems?

9. Eating—binging after the match—NO!

10. Team = Family which means any personal issues stay with us and are not shared with any members of other teams. Function as a team at all times—support each other.

11. Before you step onto the mat to wrestle, the last person you talk to is a coach—shake my hand.

    The first person you talk to after wrestling is a coach—and shake my hand—do not go stomping away, no matter what the outcome of the match is.

12. Be sure you have a good warm up—do not neglect this.

13. Follow all directions from the coaches—being coachable.

14. Help put mats away after the competition—everyone helps.

FIGURE 3-11 SECTIONAL TOURNAMENT ANNOUNCEMENTS

The post-season tournaments that act as qualifiers to your state tournament provide challenging, strenuous, and tense moments for both wrestlers and coaches. The following clear and concise announcements, made prior to the first tournament, give wrestlers the basic facts about the competition. Empowered with this information, wrestlers' tension and confusion is relieved, enabling them to focus on their individual matches.

1. Varsity is excused from class at _____ .

2. Facial hair, haircuts, fingernails, and skin will be checked at weigh-ins.

3. Weigh-ins begin on Friday at _____ and end at _____.

   Weigh-ins begin on Saturday at _____ and end at _____.

   *** You must make weight or you cannot compete.

4. Always know who you are wrestling and when—this is your job.

5. Check your bracket sheets, but recognize that changes could take place after the weigh-ins.

6. Teams entered are . . . .

7. Be dressed in uniform and warm-up on Friday by _____.

8. Show class and proper behavior—Don't put on any act whether you win or lose.

9. Tournament begins on Friday at _____.

   Tournament begins on Saturday at _____.

10. JV's turn in your uniforms now.

    Varsity, if you lose, must turn in your uniform on Saturday.

11. Number one goal: Qualify for the District Tournament!

FIGURE 3-12 POST SEASON AWARDS

EARNING A VARSITY LETTER

For any wrestler to earn a varsity letter he must compete in over one-half of varsity matches. Tournaments will count as two matches. He must also compete in the Sectional Tournament.

A wrestler could receive a varsity wrestler if the coaching staff feels this wrestler was an integral part of the team and did the best he could considering his weight class, ability, and year of graduation.

All wrestlers will be awarded Junior Varsity Awards if they do not earn a Varsity Award.

AWARDS

We will award the following trophies:

1. Most Outstanding Wrestler

   Given to the varsity wrestler who advances farthest in the state tournament; who has the best won/loss record; who has the most tournament titles; and who has demonstrated a high level of technical superiority through the season.

   Determined by the vote of the coaching staff (coaches' discretion in case of injury at post-season tournaments).

2. Most Improved Wrestler

   Given to the varsity wrestler who shows the most development from the beginning to the end of the season; who increases his won/loss record to the positive side; who earns titles or awards during the latter part of the season after failing to do so early in the season; and whose skill level makes the most improvement.

   Determined by the vote of the coaching staff.

3. Most Outstanding Junior Varsity Wrestler

   Given to the junior varsity wrestler who has the best JV won/loss record; who earns the most tournament titles or place finishes; and who possibly competed successfully in some varsity competitions (but did not earn a varsity letter).

   Determined by the vote of the coaching staff.

4. Coaches' Award

   Given to the senior wrestler who displays the most service to the sport; who maintains daily a positive attitude; who demonstrates leadership; who has high attendance; and who dedicates himself to improving his athletic skills.

   Determined by the vote of the coaching staff.

©1996 by Parker Publishing Company

FIGURE 3-12 CONTINUED

5.   Hustle Award

Given to the wrestler (either varsity or junior varsity) who displays the most intensity and commitment throughout the season; who has the most enthusiasm and spirit; and who shows the most determination to excel although his physical abilities might hinder him.

Determined by vote of the entire team.

Note: this individual cannot also be a winner of any other major awards.

FIGURE 3-13 POST SEASON LETTER TO WRESTLERS

Dear _____:

I'm glad you're reading this, and I'm betting you're eager to have a great season next year. It's time now to begin preparing for next season. Soon, winter will ask you what you've been doing all summer, so take advantage of these spring and summer months to get ready.

Ready for what?

Success. Your success. And team success. The question for us now is how to make that happen.

First, and most importantly, you need to improve your body strength. A list of exercises is included with this letter, and they're designed to do more than help you beat your grandmother at arm wrestling.

The weight room is open after school 3:00-5:00 P.M. M/W/F.

Second, you need to do some goal-setting. What do you want to accomplish next season? What are you willing to do to accomplish it? Keep in mind that to be more than mediocre, you have to do more than what everyone else is doing.

A word of caution: If you believe next year's team can be successful without any extra effort, that's a mistake. A big mistake.

Whatever you lack in talent can be made up with lots of desire, extra work, and perseverance. Confidence comes with preparation. So let's start preparing.

Preparing for success!

Your coach,

FIGURE 3-14 WRESTLER'S EVALUATION OF WRESTLING SEASON

GRADE _____ TEAM LEVEL—VARS./ JV / FRESH / MS

COACHES _____

QUESTIONS

** Circle the appropriate response to each question.

   1. How would you rate the practice facility?   Good / Fair / Poor

   2. How would you rate the uniforms/equipment?   Good / Fair / Poor

   3. Was the coach knowledgeable?   Good / Fair / Poor

   4. Were practices organized?   Good / Fair / Poor

   5. Were the coaches attentive to you?   Good / Fair / Poor

   6. Did you learn new skills to the sport?   Good / Fair / Poor

   7. Were your contests competitive for you?   Good / Fair / Poor

   8. Did you learn team-building skills?   Good / Fair / Poor

   9. Was the school administration helpful?   Good / Fair / Poor

 10. Did the coaches establish rapport?   Good / Fair / Poor

          *

 11. Will you continue in this sport next year   Yes / No

 12. *Comments*

FIGURE 3-15 WEIGHTLIFTING FOR WRESTLING

Exercises	Body Part	Purpose
Bench Press Dumbbell Flies Incline Bench Press	[Chest]	To add strength to the upper body. It applies directly to completing a double leg takedown and tight waist ride.
Bent Over Rowing (dumbbell or straight bar) Wide Grip Pull Downs Pull Ups	[Back]	To add strength to the upper and lower back. It applies directly to lifting on a high crotch lift or against an opponent's stand up.
Straight Bar Curl Dumbbell Curls Chin Ups Preacher Bench Curls	[Arms]	To add strength to the biceps and fore-arms. It applies directly to finish-ing a single leg takedown and gaining hand control on an escape.
Dips Triceps Press Forearm Curls	[Arms]	To add strength to the upper tricep and forearms. It applies directly to sustain-ing a base position and finishing a stand up escape.
Dumbbell Lateral Raise Dumbbell Forward Raise Straight Bar Upright Rows	[Shoulders]	To add strength to the shoulders. It applies directly to maintaining a proper stance while the head and shoulders are pressured by an opponent.
Squats (one day a week only)	[Legs]	To add strength to the upper and lower leg muscles. It

FIGURE 3-15 CONTINUED

Squats, *continued*

applies to stance, motion, penetration steps, and a stand up.

Key Points

1. Wrestlers should use moderate to heavy weight.

2. Each exercise should consist of 2-3 sets with 8-12 repetitions each.

3. Wrestlers should take no more than 45-90 seconds rest between sets.

4. Lifting should be done with intensity and until muscles are fatigued.

5. The entire weightlifting session should run from 30-50 minutes depending on the size of your team. To lessen the time, eliminate one exercise from each category.

6. All lifters must have a spotter and be supervised by a coach.

7. You can vary the sequence of body parts and the duration of the weightlifting session depending on the season—Pre-season, Regular Season, or Post-Season—to prevent boredom and burnout. Increase repetitions during the regular season (12-16) and lessen them during the post-season (6-8) while increasing the poundage.

8. Consult an athletic trainer for additional lifting exercises.

FIGURE 3-16 RECRUITING LETTER TO COLLEGE COACHES

Dear Coach:

Enclosed you will find information about one of my senior wrestlers who competed on the 19— varsity team. I have compiled his accomplishments on a year-by-year basis since he began competing on the varsity level.

Also included are his academic highlights, current GPA, college major preference, future plans, and other extra-curricular activities.

I believe this can assist you in any recruiting efforts you might plan regarding _____. I can also forward to you any videotapes upon request.

Thank you for any interest you show in _____, and for any further information please call me at school (phone number).

Sincerely,

FIGURE 3-17 WRESTLER'S RESUME

Resume for (Name)
His Address and Phone Number

1991-1992 (Freshman Year)
Earned Varsity letter
2nd in Conference Tournament
District Qualifier
14-8 Record (5 pins) at 145 lbs.
Achieved Academic Honor Roll

1992-1993 (Sophomore Year)
Earned Varsity letter
2nd at Richmond Heights Invitational
2nd at Sectional Tournament
1st in Conference Tournament
District Semifinalist
18-5 Record (10 pins) at 152 lbs.
Led the team in Escapes
Achieved Academic Honor Roll

1993-1994 (Junior Year)
Earned Varsity letter
3rd in Div. III State Tournament
District Champion
Sectional Champion
Conference Champion
Richmond Hts. Invitational Champion
Team Captain
Coaches' Award Winner
25-3 Record (16 pins) at 167 lbs.
Led the team in Nearfalls and Escapes
Inducted into National Honor Society
Junior Class Vice-President
Scholar-Athlete Award Winner

1994-1995 (Senior Year)
Varsity letter winner
Varsity Team Captain
State Champion
District Champion
Sectional Champion
Conference Champion
Richmond Hts. Invitational Champion
Lincoln Hts. Invitational Champion
30-0 Record (21 pins) at 167 lbs.
Led team in Nearfalls and Takedowns
Most Outstanding Wrestler Award
Senior Class President
NHS Vice-President
Scholar-Athlete Award Winner
Varsity letter winner in Football
News Herald Wrestler of the Year

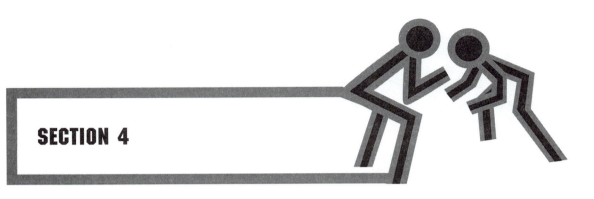

SECTION 4

Motivation

All coaches love the self-motivated athlete. Unfortunately, relatively few wrestlers have the self-motivation to give maximum effort when they believe that only minimum effort is needed. A common lament of many coaches is that their wrestlers are unmotivated, that they don't work hard enough, and that they're not willing to sacrifice to achieve success. "Why aren't they motivated?" they complain. "Don't they want to win?"

Furthermore, too many coaches expect that the wrestlers who arrive for that first practice are already motivated since they have decided to give up time after school to participate. It is a common mistake to take motivation for granted. Coaches need to understand (1) what motivates athletes to participate in any sport; (2) how athletes stay motivated; and (3) how motivation influences athletic performance. Walt Kelly's Pogo understood the concept succinctly: "We have met the enemy, and he is *us*."

WHAT IS MOTIVATION?

In his book, *Coaching and Motivation*, William Warren makes clear distinctions between the perspectives that coaches and athletes have about motivation: "To coaches, motivation means finding ways to get players to do things they might not want to do on their own; to players, motivation means having reasons for acting or failing to act." Coaches may rely more on extrinsic motivation (praise or rewards) while athletes, who may enjoy and benefit from the coach's acknowledgement, focus on their intrinsic needs when defining motivation.

The act of motivating is in its simplest terms a means of fostering a strong belief in you and your program. You establish this belief by the sincerity of what you say and the intensity of how you say it. Motivation can, at times, be the kind of *image* you wish to reflect—strong, decisive, smart, responsible, etc.—and you have got to work at that image (like a public relations firm does for a client corporation); you need to work at the *quality* of your image which, in turn, can prompt wrestlers to:

1. maximize their efforts in practice and matches;

2. be enthusiastic about their place on the squad;

3. maintain persistence toward a specified goal;

4. handle obstacles, failures, and criticism without quitting the team;

5. be intense during a competition;

6. improve their physical and mental skills in wrestling;

7. display a positive attitude;

8. be attentive and alert during practices and contests;

9. express an enjoyment for practicing and competing; and

10. work cooperatively with teammates and the entire coaching staff.

Motivation designed on an extrinsic level can get wrestlers *addicted* to the sport, and the means to achieve that certainly vary from athlete to athlete. Motivation, therefore, should be individualized for best results.

You can capitalize on the wrestler's intrinsic motivation by challenging him to learn new techniques, avoiding punishment if he fails to master them, and tolerating his mistakes, since errors are natural to any learning process. Work, then, to eliminate those errors through drill sessions and instruction. Your personal expectations for each wrestler also have much to do with his level of motivation.

The coach needs to set up the circumstances and conditions that prompt wrestlers to act on their personal motivations. Furthermore, motivation is closely linked to emotion. Truly, the wrestling coach is a salesman: selling a love for the sport, dialoging about its benefits, inviting athletes to participate, and offering them rewards for that participation. You are always meeting and challenging the personal needs they bring to the sport. Coaching *is* motivating.

If motivation is a psychological stimulus that can prompt wrestlers to perform their best in competitions, then the coach has to begin by studying his wrestlers' mental approach to competing. The coach has to analyze the wrestlers' psyches:

☑What are their personal interests?

☑Why have they chosen to become members of the team?

☑How committed are they to the program?

☑What has motivated them in the past?

☑What motivational strategies have failed on them in the past?

☑How do they handle adversity?

WHAT DOES RESEARCH SAY ABOUT PRIMARY MOTIVATIONAL FORCES?

What are the key factors that prompt athletes to become motivated to compete successfully? Recent research has identified some primary motivational forces. They are not listed here in any order of importance. Athletes are motivated to:

☑demonstrate individual excellence;

☑help the team win;

☑improve self-esteem;

☑prove oneself in competition;

☑overcome fear (especially the fear of failure);

☑release tension and/or anxiety;

☑dominate others; and

☑gain approval from peers.

Note the intrinsic foundation of these items which are common to all of us. The coach's challenge, therefore, is to create the circumstances and conditions in the practice room that capitalize on these intrinsic motivations.

WHAT DOES RESEARCH SAY ABOUT SOURCES OF MOTIVATION?

Dr. Robert Weinberg surveyed junior and senior high school age athletes and discovered the following sources of motivation rated from most to least popular:

Affiliation—the desire to socialize and make friends

Excellence—the intrinsic need to do one's best

Success—the extrinsic need to gain rewards

Power—the desire to have influence over others

Aggression—the need to dominate others

Stress—the enjoyment of pressure associated with competition

Independence—"I did it on my own"

In a 1987 study of 26,300 students ages 10-18, Dr. Martha Ewing and Dr. Vern Seefeldt, professors at Michigan State University, discovered that athletes stayed motivated when they (1) enjoyed the sport; (2) sustained friendships; (3) increased their physical fitness; (4) enjoyed the competition; and (5) achieved success. Finally, a 1990 survey by the Athletic Footwear Association asked 20,000 kids why they participated in sports, and the number one answer was to have fun.

In contrast, athletes chose to quit when they experienced (1) an incompetent coach; (2) poor relations with teammates; (3) communication problems with the coach; and (4) the accomplishment of their goal(s).

A clinical study of an eastern university hockey team that had suffered chronic losing seasons revealed that the detailed use of the following strategies enabled the team to earn a winning record and make the playoffs. The players experienced . . .

☑positive feedback about their efforts;

☑praise for even minor accomplishments;

☑constant dialogue with their coaches and fellow athletes;

☑appropriate goal setting; and

☑their individual results and statistics posted publicly.

WHAT DOES RESEARCH SAY ABOUT MOTIVATIONAL METHODS?

To be sure, there are many ways to motivate, and different wrestlers are motivated in different ways. Even success isn't always a motivator. There are, however, several essential factors linked to motivation that can influence any wrestler's desire to compete successfully.

The degree of motivation may vary from wrestler to wrestler, but each one is entitled to the same acceptance, respect, and concern. No matter what their physical talents or mental skills, whether they routinely struggle in competitions or often achieve victory, they deserve the coach's complete attention. No wrestler deserves mediocre attention from the coach.

First, wrestlers need feedback. This could occur through a private or team discussion about their progress, a critique of their techniques, or praise for their efforts. You could give your wrestlers weekly, or possibly daily, notification of their development through posted charts or statistics (see Figure 4-1).

The coach should provide specific information about performances (practice or competition) to the wrestler, especially the one who has set his own training goals. This constant assessment (beyond generic commentary, for example, like "You did a nice job today" or "That was a good takedown") encourages wrestlers to set personal standards for their practice and, hence, the competition. Better, more specific compliments would be, "You never stopped hustling during your matches today. You're setting a standard I'd like everyone to follow. Well done!" or "Your finish on your single leg was excellent. Do it that way all the time and no one will stop it." In fact, they should be given some indications of their improvement after each practice.

Second, positive praise is important, especially for the wrestlers who are junior varsity. They are as important to any program as the superstars. Certainly they have to learn to "pay their dues." They should, however, be treated with as much attention and respect as the varsity. Being straightforward with wrestlers often promotes a better relationship and rapport, and in the case of marginal wrestlers well-phrased compliments enhance their sense of belonging and self-esteem.

James "Doc" Counsilman motivated his Indiana University swimmers by maintaining a positive attitude around them, giving them public recognition, helping them see their progress towards their goals, working to build their self-esteem, and fostering team unity. His players felt secure in their positions on the team and welcomed challenges.

Third, increase the wrestlers' knowledge base and physical conditioning. The more they know about that sport's specific techniques and strategies, the more confident they'll feel about competing. Be sure to point out examples when their physical conditioning has produced favorable results for them.

Fourth, discover and exploit each wrestler's level of aspiration. What are their goals? What are they shooting for? The coach's job here is to assist the wrestler in setting a goal(s) that is both difficult and reachable. Assess each wrestler's level of motivation by having them complete a personal questionnaire early in the season (see Figure 4-2).

The coach needs to give logical and practical reflection on how he wants to motivate his wrestlers in order to bring forth something within them that they didn't know they had. This requires careful planning and creative strategies.

How do wrestlers stay motivated? Let them tell you:

"I get motivated when I'm pushed to try my hardest by the coaches. They never give up on me, no matter what my wrestling ability is."

"I keep participating when the coach makes me feel good about myself, when he makes it fun."

"I'm motivated by a coach who has knowledge of the sport and is able to communicate this to us in an intense way that is still fun and interesting."

"A motivational coach won't let you quit, even if you aren't good at the sport."

"I get motivated when the coach is able to relate to his wrestlers. He has to be the kind of guy who is able to have his wrestlers wrestle like champions all the time."

"I'm motivated when I'm pushed beyond my limits. I like competing because it brings out the best in everyone. My coaches have encouraged me to strive to be the best."

"He should talk in an encouraging manner instead of yelling. He should only talk positive."

"I love to compete. My family was into sports, especially wrestling. I think you have to be dedicated and intense."

"It's important that the coach is more than a coach, he's a friend, too. He has to understand me and discipline me."

"The coach has to be in control and have the ability to motivate me. Motivation to succeed is the most important thing a wrestler can have and probably the hardest thing a coach can teach."

"I don't get motivated by coaches who are always angry. They have to be fun at times, and they have to be a friend."

"To motivate me, the coach has to be able to give constructive *criticism and encouragement, not sarcasm."*

"I appreciate the fact that my coach made me work hard until I got it right and helped me fix what I was doing wrong. He worked with the whole team and each individual wrestler."

"My parents originally motivated me with my sports, but now Coach McGrain has probably made the biggest difference because he always pushes you to make yourself better. He never looks at one individual, he is always worried about the team. He's caring but tough."

"I feed off the smell of victory."

"I love competition, and I want to stay in shape. That's what motivates me. During the summer I set a goal to get in 200 hours of work. I got in 241 hours. My coach helped a lot. He always has a positive attitude—he's very optimistic, very motivational."

"I'm motivated by performing well in front of a big crowd. I like being a part of the competition."

"I get motivated when I know the coach is concerned about every athlete on the team from the best to the worst. A coach has to be like a second father who can teach you about sports and life."

"I'm motivated when I know that the coach is concerned about me as an athlete but also as a student. He has to be straightforward with you and not feed you some line. He has to look out for you but not pamper you. When I came out of mid-

dle school, I was the top dog and I kind of had a big head. My coach set me straight and got me going in the right direction. He also let me know that there was more to life than wrestling."

The wrestling coach needs to stress improvement, not wins or losses. And keep in mind that motivational strategies used at the beginning of the season should probably differ from the motivation used near the middle or end of the season.

Motivation in pressure situations also needs to be addressed here. Preparing for any competition is seldom fun for wrestlers because it normally involves extensive physical and mental effort. Display an "I care" attitude and be ready to acknowledge those who maintain a positive outlook through the grind of practice. Make practice more appealing by placing your wrestlers in situations that lead to success and that build their confidence.

Finally, remain ethical—do not offer money or gifts as rewards for their participation or performance. You need to carefully consider the incentives you could provide that could motivate your wrestlers. Their age, maturity level, interests, and culture are important here.

WHAT ARE THE STRATEGIES THAT STIMULATE ATHLETES?

Do you see yourself as a Vince Lomardi or a Knute Rockne? Should you use gimmicks and theatrics to motivate your wrestlers? Should today's coach act like a cheerleader for his wrestlers? Consider these questions when deciding how to inspire your kids. Keep in mind the differences between inspiration and motivation.

"Yelling doesn't win ball games. It doesn't put any points on the scoreboard. And I don't think words win ball games all the time. Players do. Preparation does."

—(FROM JERRY TARKANIAN)

Whatever strategies you eventually employ, be sure to maintain your own identity and style when inspiring wrestlers. Second, gimmicks can be effective if not overdone. Finally, you need to be supportive and involved as a coach, but never lose your focus during a practice or match.

As a teacher and coach I am always willing to try any strategy that can motivate my students and athletes. Based on Weinberg's research and my own experiences, I've designed 101 ways to motivate wrestlers (in fact, any athlete). I've categorized these strategies into divisions for coaches who have detected certain areas where their team lacks motivation. Once you have identified where your team is experiencing a breakdown in motivation you can employ the specific strategies outlined below.

101 Ways to Motivate Your Wrestlers

Affiliation: Does my team fail to cooperate, behave, or act like a team? Does my team lack positive social interaction?

1. Smile a lot.

2. Tell your wrestlers what motivates you, then model being a motivated person.

3. Remain positive, especially through setbacks.

4. Never use physical coercion as a motivator.

5. Congratulate each wrestler for choosing to participate.

6. Consider each wrestler's personality—the type of special guidance he needs—and listen to him.

7. Treat each wrestler with respect and affection.

8. Treat wrestlers consistently and fairly.

9. Show enthusiasm and a positive attitude constantly.

10. Set the mood you want the players to adopt and always be under control.

11. Send birthday cards to them.

12. Visit the wrestlers and their families at their homes.

13. Make phone calls to the wrestlers' parents where you thank and acknowledge them for their contributions.

14. Be sure the coaches speak to every wrestler by his first name at every practice.

15. Attend another school function together—another sport's "big" game or a play.

16. Go out to dinner together.

17. Go to a movie together.

18. Always be ready to counsel wrestlers about personal problems.

19. Have your more mature senior wrestlers act as mentors for younger ones (the "buddy system").

20. Go on "retreat" together (camping, canoeing, swimming, hiking, etc.) or work on a community project.

21. Go to a college wrestling match together.

Commitment to Excellence: Does my team fail to strive to practice and compete to their very best? Do they represent themselves as truly top-notch competitors?

22. Discover and then promote team leaders.

23. Put motivational slogans and sayings on the walls of the locker room and practice room.

24. Invite alumni to speak to the wrestlers the day before a competition.

25. Invite popular teachers to speak to the wrestlers before a practice.

26. Ask other coaches to talk to and encourage the wrestlers who also compete on their teams.

27. Ask any local celebrities to speak to the team.

28. Use a display case for the wrestlers' pictures and the team roster (see Figure 4-3 on highlighting team and individual accomplishments).

29. Display the wrestlers' statistics in the locker room.

30. Have cheerleaders or managers put up signs and slogans in the school's hallways to promote matches.

31. Speak about team and individual pride.

32. Tape inspirational messages in their lockers or have them delivered to them during the school day.

Organization: Does my team practice and compete under control? Do the team, parents, and administration recognize and accept the value of the practice schedule, the school property, and the team goals?

33. Be organized, especially regarding time management.

34. Establish rules for the good of the team, then follow them.

35. Order stylish uniforms.

36. Keep your facilities clean and attractive.

37. Travel in style and surprise the team by traveling to the big match in limousines.

38. Get school administrators to commend the team during a school assembly.

39. Request local politicians to support and praise the team by composing official proclamations that commend any of the team's accomplishments.

40. Conduct home meets in an impressive manner.

41. Get the wrestlers' names in the newspaper and then send a thank you note for their coverage.

42. Get their names and the team's accomplishments on radio and then thank the station.

43. Invite local television stations to do brief profiles on the team as a whole or on some outstanding wrestlers.

44. Utilize the school's public address system each week.

45. Send out a newsletter that profiles the team and your wrestlers' individual accomplishments.

46. Design, develop, and distribute a media guide.

47. Have a post season awards banquet (possibly at a local restaurant).

48. Use videos of the team's practice performances.

49. Show videos or films of outstanding college wrestlers in action (highlight films).

50. Have a "Meet the Team" night for parents and the media.

51. Put pictures of the wrestlers on the windows or doors of community businesses.

52. Honor or create special traditions associated with the team (for example, having an alumni or hall of fame match where you honor former wrestlers).

53. Bring back former wrestlers to teach their special techniques that enabled them to be successful.

54. Arrange dramatic pep assemblies.

55. Put signs in their yards.

56. Develop a strong base of supporters for the team (the booster club or parents' group).

57. Have a "Parents' Night" for a competition where wrestlers are introduced with their parents.

58. Speak to any local civic groups about the team.

59. Be visible in the community.

60. Have cheerleaders send good luck notes to the wrestlers.

61. Help senior wrestlers get into college (applications, scholarships, letters of recommendation, etc.).

62. Design and distribute a team poster/calendar.

63. Invite lettermen and/or team captains to speak at pep assemblies or to any school organization.

64. Order team hats.

65. Order warm up tops or sweatshirts that have their names on the back.

66. Post news articles about your wrestling team.

Success and Mastery: Does my team fall short of accomplishing goals? Are they failing to produce the results I know they're capable of?

67. Support the wrestler's academic obligations (even assist with any of his subjects if you can).

68. Use a variety of drills during practice.

69. Set daily goals, often associated with mastering certain techniques and skills.

70. Set weekly goals that could relate to the upcoming contest.

71. Set seasonal goals as a team.

72. Have a pre-planned response for potential failures.

73. Start and end practice on time.

74. Don't be afraid to give a day off.

75. Be sure that each wrestler knows he is making a strong contribution to the team.

76. Tell wrestlers to expect positive outcomes.

77. Change the practice routine or the warm up.

78. Don't make excessive demands and be flexible.

79. Be sure your wrestlers are physically prepared for competition.

80. Give wrestlers books that deal with positive thinking and optimistic attitudes.

81. Allow wrestlers time during practice to do what they want to do to make themselves better competitors.

Challenges: Does my team avoid challenges both in practice and competition? Does pressure rob them of their ability to compete successfully?

82. Challenge the team but have reasonable expectations for them.

83. Offer concrete goals that are expressed in simple terms, e.g., "Let's earn ____ more takedowns in our next match."

84. Avoid pressurized goals, e.g., "We *have* to win this one."

85. Have fun—at practice and at the competition. Develop a sense of humor.

86. Play a fun game at the end of practice.

87. Organize drills into fun and challenging competitions.

88. Use current, popular music during practice.

Power: Does my team demonstrate a lack of confidence? Does my team suffer from a lack of competitiveness?

89. Show your wrestlers the correspondences you get from college coaches.

90. Make sure everyone has a chance to compete.

91. Offer awards (certificates, for example) for the top performance at practice each week.

92. Offer an award (a t-shirt, for example) for the top performance (not necessarily a victorious one) at the most recent competition.

93. Don't let any wrestler make excuses or rationalize a defeat.

94. Don't let wrestlers blame others for any defeats or failures.

95. Tell your wrestlers any praise the team receives from opposing coaches.

96. Describe the positive feelings associated with successful competitions.

97. Be especially attentive towards wrestlers who appear to be discouraged or unhappy.

98. Have them listen to tapes of motivational speakers.

99. Teach them how to visualize success.

100. Keep your wrestlers focused on their accomplishments and not their failures

101. Be creative.

Be cautious and selective about using professional athletes as examples of motivation. Their reasons for competing (money, fame) can certainly differ from your athletes,' so cite only the most appropriate professionals when illustrating motivation for your wrestlers.

The coach should set the example. He will probably be the most motivated individual on the team and, therefore, should exhibit each day the traits of a motivated person. How you *act* and what you *say* should always reflect motivational signals to your wrestlers.

At issue here is the type of praise you give your wrestlers. Know when to praise a little and when to praise a lot. You need to recognize that too much praise lessens the impact, value and sincerity of your message. Concentrate on specific praise, which promotes independent action, when individuals deserve it and generic praise to prompt the entire team to act in a certain manner.

WHAT IS THE LINK BETWEEN COMMUNICATION AND MOTIVATION?

Effective motivation clearly stems from effective communication, but communication must be more than talking. You also have to listen and comprehend. The wrestler needs to see your level of communication equal your level of concern. Allow them to communicate as well. Invite them to provide input into any plans for the program, and then discuss the contribution they want to make. Here, you are setting up the conditions of their commitment. Sometimes, this can be accomplished through a personal conference with the wrestler where you can also discover much about his health, family, grades, and motivation.

Clearly, coaching requires communication. The coach needs to consider how he transmits messages and how athletes interpret them. Effective communication and, in turn, effective motivation can be hindered by:

☑ poor verbal skills by the coach;

☑ wrestlers who don't pay attention;

☑ wrestlers who don't understand verbal cues;

☑ messages that are inconsistent; and

☑ an environment that threatens open dialogue.

Most instances of communication occur when coaches tell their wrestlers what they're doing *wrong*. In fact, these instances are often characterized by vague statements like, "C'mon, try again. Do it right," "What's wrong with you?", "That's not how to do it," or "C'mon, *think*."

Instead, coaches would get better results if they provided exact information about the correct technique or behavior. They should be more concerned with teaching than judging, especially with those wrestlers who may already have low self-esteem. When wrestlers hear judgmental language they often become tense and uneasy, even defensive. Any worries they may have about reaching their potential become magnified.

When communicating, also be an effective listener:

☑ Be accessible to listening by giving adequate time to hear what the wrestler wants to say.

☑ Focus intensely on what he says.

☑ Repeat the message as you understand it and see if your understanding is correct—for example, "What I hear you saying is . . . ."

☑Don't interrupt the wrestler.

☑Hold back any emotional response.

This is active listening, as opposed to passive, silent listening. Here, you interact with the wrestler by providing him with a paraphrased response that proves you understand what he has said. And don't neglect those physical mannerisms that make up non-verbal communication: head and hand movements, gestures, touching, body position, even the tone of your voice are all associated with any act of verbal communication.

Overall, to keep wrestlers motivated, the coach has to make them feel special to the team. Their personal achievements have to be recognized and praised. They have to know that the coach cares about them personally and that they are making an important contribution to helping the team achieve its goals. It's also okay to brag about their accomplishments in the school and in the community.

WHAT MAKES A WRESTLER WANT TO QUIT?

Here, a variety of factors can be involved, some of which you cannot alter. However, the concerned coach can deal effectively with the wrestler troubled by the mental or physical strains of the sport.

Often, quitting occurs when the wrestler is struggling with failure. A knowledgeable and caring coach should recall a positive moment for him and review it with him. Encourage him to stay involved until he has won at least once. Don't lie to him or give false praise, but certainly point out improvement.

Regarding the physical demands of the sport that may be overwhelming the wrestler, the coach needs to explain that the wrestler isn't alone. All athletes, even the great ones, hate the physical punishment required in preparing to compete.

Sometimes wrestlers quit because the satisfaction and reward of wearing the uniform is overshadowed by the realization that they are obligated to work harder than they ever have before in order to put on that uniform. These kind of wrestlers need to understand that hard work produces success, but not necessarily wins.

"If it weren't for the dark days, we wouldn't
know what it is to walk in the light."

—(FROM EARL CAMPBELL, FORMER NFL FULLBACK)

Clearly, there are many more reasons why wrestlers quit than can be expressed in a single chapter, yet the more prominent ones will be highlighted here. Quitting often is not an individual decision made by the wrestler. Others—family, friends, teachers—may have influenced it. Overall, wrestlers choose to quit when . . .

☑their peers tell them to;

☑they resent their teammates;

☑they resent or distrust the coach;

☑alcohol or drugs have become more important;

☑wrestling is no longer enjoyable (burn out);

☑family problems interfere;

☑they fear injury or the physical grind; or

☑academic problems surface.

When pressed up against themselves, many athletes decide to quit to relieve the burden of confronting their own inadequacies.

What should the coach do?

Initially, you should try to talk out the problem. Sometimes, the wrestler has set such a difficult goal that the challenge to accomplish it has overwhelmed him. You can help set a more realistic goal and encourage persistence to reach it. The root cause will always relate to one (or several) of his intrinsic motivational needs that is not being satisfied.

If it is failure that is interfering, model how to cope with failure and emphasize skill improvement, rather than winning. Clarify and highlight those moments when the wrestler has been successful and allow him to "savor" those achievements. Don't nag the wrestler about his decision, but certainly involve his parents. Invite them and any other athletes to talk to the wrestler. Above all, keep a positive, patient attitude.

HOW CAN PEP TALKS PUMP THEM UP?

When many coaches consider their pre-game locker room pep talk, they get a vision of Knute Rockne's "Win this one for the Gipper" speech. Such drama doesn't motivate all athletes (many times it isn't even needed) and in fact it can be counter-productive. Pep talks need not be emotional tirades. More often, they should be business-like in tone and format where the coach expresses clearly and as briefly as possible what awaits the wrestlers and what is expected of them. Whether the coach wants to provoke his athletes or not, he should be straightforward and honest. The coach must demonstrate calmness and confidence, especially when the wrestlers seem tense or uncertain. You can use emotion, however, if the timing seems right.

An effective pep talk has a theme. Expressing a specific, straightforward message is important. It could be about perseverance, poise, or points. You decide the subject, select the words, give an illustration to help them understand, and be sure they're attentive.

Eliminate distractions. In the locker room, don't give the pep talk when they're dressing, listening to music, or adjusting their uniform or headgear. Athletes should be seated, relaxed, and quiet.

Avoid impromptu pep talks. Most of these are doomed to fail. Nor should the coach embarrass himself, any player, or assistant coach as an excuse to inspire the team as a whole. Don't make promises (like to shave your head or run behind the bus) since such stunts lead more to amusement than motivation.

Select language and/or gimmicks carefully. Keith Dambrot lost his job as basketball coach at Central Michigan University for using the word "nigger" to motivate his black players. He believed the word conveyed the "positive qualities of toughness, determination, perseverance and character." The racial epithet, Dambrot believed, had more to do with his close relationship with his players and his style of coaching than with the abuse that university officials accused him of. "I wanted to be their friend," Dambrot explained. "We don't view ourselves as white and black. We view ourselves as family. I'm a victim of having been around players who used that term in a positive way around me. Plus, I've allowed them to say things to me that other people might term offensive." Central Michigan administrators fired Dambrot anyway.

A Florida football coach staged a fake shooting of himself during a pep talk in the school cafeteria. After players fled in horror and three police cars raced to the school, he admitted that the stunt was "poorly contrived. What a gross mistake." That night his team lost the game 27-14. The coach explained, "Football demands so much physically, mentally and spiritually, that was an attempt to motivate them to perform over their limits." The school superintendent disagreed: "It is my opinion that using a weapon of any sort—whether it's real or not—is totally inappropriate."

Involve others in the pep talk. There's also no rule that says the coach must be the one to always give the pep talk. Community leaders, former wrestlers, popular teachers, or interested administrators can speak to the wrestlers before a competition or practice. Even better, wrestlers can give each other pep talks if the coach guides them correctly through that process.

Several times during my own coaching tenure I have worked with other coaches to have their champion players dialogue with my wrestlers. Once, I arranged for the girls on the volleyball team, who had won several league titles in a row, to speak one on one with my wrestlers who were preparing for their league tournament. The volleyball coach and I paired them up, gave them space to talk privately after practice the day before the tournament, and let them do the rest. The kids talked to each other about competing, pressure, and winning. These young people talked seriously and formally with one another about their feelings and responsibilities as athletes. It was a marvelous experience for both the players and the coaches. Though expected to finish near the bottom, that team placed second in the tournament.

Getting wrestlers "psyched up" has its rewards and its faults. One wrestler may need a high level of arousal while another performs better when the motivation is more low-key. Each wrestler's arousal level needs to be evaluated; personality, attitude, and maturity need to be assessed. If the wrestler has an introverted personality or is an experienced competitor, less psyching is usually recommended. You shouldn't, however, neglect his motivational needs so that he becomes indifferent towards the competition.

What about after the competition? Many coaches favor a brief lecture in the locker room or bus after a competition where the match is analyzed and performances discussed. I do not. I believe that after any competition, especially one that has been rigorous or disappointing, the wrestler cares little for any commentary. If you must do this, make it only a quick, objective analysis of the competition. Make only positive comments, for if they've wrestled badly they'll know it. You can use this moment to remind them of the next day's schedule (the time of practice or the next match) and to congratulate the performance of any individual(s). A wise coach can also use this time to discover if there are any injuries.

Remain positive after a competition (and prompt the kids to stay positive, too). Over time you'll get better results if you praise and reward rather than criticize and punish. Remember to be realistic about your expectations of your wrestlers. And if any part of your motivation includes a promised reward—a steak dinner, for example—for a victory, then be sure to follow through on it promptly. Live up to your word, especially if a matter of discipline is at hand.

At times you may prefer to motivate only individuals; in other instances, the team should be the focus of your commendation. Decide what kind of awards or praise you may deliver in either instance.

"Motivation is something . . . that is a constant desire to do your very best at all times and under any circumstances."

—(FROM JOE DIMAGGIO)

HOW CAN THE COACH CREATE ENTHUSIASM AND PRIDE?

In conclusion, motivation may be a mystery to many of us, but we should not neglect its importance. When coaches motivate effectively, they develop enthusiasm and pride in their wrestlers, who can pass these traits onto the younger guys. Proper motivation keeps wrestlers committed to the program and excited about competing.

Coaches need to recognize that some wrestlers shuffle passively towards competitions while others strut with overconfidence, and it can be a struggle to motivate wrestlers who lack commitment to you, the program, or their teammates. However, if you identify and promote their intrinsic needs they can be productive members of your program and achieve their individual potential. You must be willing to be flexible—i.e., giving the squad a heated pep talk one day and simply patting one kid's back the next. You should also discuss motivation with swimming and cross country coaches since, like us, they deal with preparing athletes for individual competitions.

Motivating kids takes work. It takes creative thinking. It must be continuous. That is why the coach himself has to be motivated. Your wrestlers deserve that above all else.

"More enduringly than any other sport, wrestling teaches self-control and pride. Some have wrestled without great skill; none have wrestled without pride."

—(FROM DAN GABLE)

FIGURE 4-1 STATISTICS CHART

VARSITY WRESTLING STATISTICS

VS. _____ DATE _____

WT. NAME	RECORD	TD	ESC	REV	NF	PINS	TEAM PTS.
103							
112							
119							
125							
130							
135							
140							
145							
152							
160							
171							
189							
215							
HWT							

COMMENTS

FIGURE 4-2 MOTIVATION QUESTIONNAIRE

Name _____ Grade _____

Study Hall Periods _____ Lunch Period _____ HR _____

1. What will make wrestling fun for you this year?

2. What could be a great achievement for you this season?
   What is possible for you?

3. How would you like the coaches to motivate you? How can the coaches help you be successful?

4. What *really* motivates you?

5. Why makes wrestling an exciting sport for you?

FIGURE 4-3 HIGHLIGHT TEAM/INDIVIDUAL ACCOMPLISHMENTS

Trophies won in tournaments should have a prominent place in school display cases.

Put pictures of state champion wrestlers above the display case. This helps for quick recognition when you invite them to correspond with an athlete in the school or to teach a technique to the team.

FIGURE 4-3 CONTINUED

In the wrestling room display boards or placards that identify previous qualifiers to the state tournament.

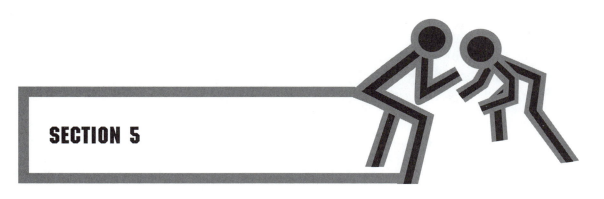

SECTION 5

The Coach's Duties

John Thompson of Georgetown University states: "I tell the kids that it's as though we're putting on a play. I'm the director. I'm going to pick the script, and I'm going to give them their roles. They're the actors. Their job is to learn those roles—that's what practice is about. When we go out on the court, that's our stage. Out there they're supposed to perform as we practiced. I don't want anybody making up new lines, putting on their own act."

Dr. Patricia Lucas, Principal of Manatee High School in Bradenton, Florida says: "I always hire a teacher who can coach rather than a coach who may or may not be a good teacher. The classroom performance must be credible first. Usually, an excellent teacher will be an excellent coach. Coaches occupy a unique position with students, often spending more time with them than their parents do. This opportunity to make a positive contribution to a young person's life is a serious responsibility."

According to Joe Namath, "To be a leader, you have to make people want to follow you, and nobody wants to follow someone who doesn't know where he's going."

THE HEAD COACH

When you become a head wrestling coach you are expected to be a skilled clinician, a competent administrator, and an effective counselor. Many of us work from dawn to dusk planning practices and repairing equipment, meeting with administrators and reviewing videotapes, instructing athletes and conducting drills, scouting opponents and dialoguing with parents. Such tasks can easily overwhelm even the most energetic person.

And how are we evaluated?

For many of us the competition is our evaluation—an evaluation that shows up in one of two columns: Wins or Losses. Let me offer, instead, a more effective and worthwhile criteria for evaluating your achievement: *Total your number of successful relationships, not your wins and losses.*

If you focus your efforts on building positive relationships with your wrestlers, their parents, school administrators, fellow coaches, league opponents, and support personnel, team and individual success surely follows. Indeed, when the entire coaching staff concerns themselves with developing successful relationships, team achievement and personal accomplishment are maximized. This happens because a supportive, goal-oriented network has been established where everyone involved in the program seeks to benefit someone else.

Creating these kinds of relationships depends on knowing first the interests, experiences, and skills of your wrestlers. Why did they join wrestling? In what other clubs or sports are they involved? What are their talents? Discover the background of each wrestler and build on it.

Learn the names of your wrestlers' parents, the parents' occupations, brothers and sisters, maybe even how they all spent their summer vacations. When you take an active interest in each wrestler's family, that family takes an active interest in your program. Talk to parents after matches, during the "down" times at tournaments, at another sporting event. As you use those brief opportunities to befriend them, allow them to get to know you.

Furthermore, you have to form relationships with your colleagues and administrators. Be sure they know your concern for the wrestlers' academics and behavior in school. Invite them to the competitions (offer free tickets if you have to) and solicit their advice on dealing with certain kids in the program. In short, involve them by teaching them how they can make a positive contribution to the wrestling program.

Not only must the head coach work to create supportive relations with the wrestlers, parents, and administrators, he also has to develop positive associations with match officials. Too often, this relationship has been seen as confrontational where intense coaches perceive an official's neutral demeanor as indifference. Coaches should consider the time and dedication invested by the officials in their profession to conduct matches efficiently, competently, and fairly.

The head coach must be the catalyst for this relationship-building process. He must be very attentive to encouraging first his own staff, then the wrestlers, parents, administrators, and other personnel to adopt the goals important to the program. Everyone directly involved with the program must accept the validity and value of the team's objectives. This takes, to be sure, much time and effort (sometimes almost an entire season), but the ultimate reward is the faith all these individuals have in the coach and his program.

As discussed in Section 1, the bricks that make up the foundation of the wrestling program are the head coach's personal principles. These principles determine the decisions he makes, the goals he has, and the attitude he expresses. An important principle is humility. When the match is over wrestlers should bow their heads in victory or hold them high in defeat.

Another significant principle is respect. Wrestlers should be taught to respect without exception coaches, teammates, teachers, classmates, opponents, administrators, and especially themselves. If they're demonstrating respect they're demonstrating dignity. Sometimes, kids may feel that a loss is also an excuse to dismiss self-respect and antagonize others. Losing and winning, they must understand, have nothing to do with respect. That behavior should remain unchanged no matter what the match outcome is.

"I think the most important thing in life and in playing any sport is to try and do the very best that you possibly can at all times. Always remember that no matter what you achieve in life, if you try a little harder, if you make that second effort, you can achieve more."

—(FROM HANK AARON)

The head coach must assemble a staff where everyone supports each other and shares the same vision for the program. Although these individuals may possess different personalities, everyone must respect each other, deal cooperatively with challenges and problems, and assist the head coach in a loyal and enthusiastic manner.

As the head coach prompts his staff to be energized and motivated throughout the season, he also must work diligently to achieve his own potential as a leader and a role model. You should always try to improve your ability as a leader and boost your staff's enthusiasm. You must be prepared, though, to deal with tardiness, conflicts, and emotions. Overall, your style of leadership must be consistent and confident.

As the head coach, attempt to present yourself more as a leader than a boss. Maintain your credibility and status by working hard to create an environment that fosters mutual support between you and your assistants. Problem solving is easier when a group is involved. Collaboration directed towards solutions rather than complaints enables the entire team to produce more during practices and competitions. Obviously, some "give and take" can occur when disagreements happen, but a mature, goal-oriented staff whose members are as ready to listen as they are to talk can accept this.

Effective leadership hinges on your ability to perform successfully in both personal and professional situations. Here are ten tips for improving your interpersonal relations with colleagues and kids:

1. Never ignore others. This type of behavior lowers their morale and suggests your are apathetic.

2. Present opportunities for dialogues and then listen attentively. Sometimes, subordinates may feel uncertain about approaching you with their ideas or concerns. Don't be so wrapped up in your own agenda that you tune out.

3. Apologize immediately when you've hurt someone. Follow up with a note of apology and possibly a small gift.

4. Follow through on all promises.

5. Recognize when others' personal problems are affecting their performance and assist them in eliminating those problems (counseling).

6. When critiquing others either formally or informally begin by having them do a self-evaluation. This precludes any defensive behavior on their part and sets up better communication overall.

7. Present an image of calm self-confidence but avoid being "pushy." People function best around leaders who appear strong, positive, and relaxed even during difficult situations.

8. Encourage innovative thinking by posing questions. For example: "How should we finish our single leg takedown from this position?" or "Why didn't our stand ups work in our last match?" Discourage negative thinking like "That will never work!" with "Maybe before it didn't, but today is different."

9. Insist on plain, honest feedback. Admit you don't have all the answers and be open to change. This helps build others' self-esteem and commitment.

10. Empathize with your colleagues and wrestlers. Keep in mind that physical coordination, attention span, and commitment levels vary from person to person, especially in younger athletes. Imagine yourself in their shoes before offering a criticism or complaint.

In the professional, administrative domain the head coach must always be organized. Time management is especially important. Each day you should list your priorities and your schedule (a calendar can help) and then follow through (see Figure 5-1). There are, of course, many typical duties for a head wrestling coach to accomplish.

Typical Duties for the Head Coach

1. Organization and administration of entire program

2. Practice instruction

3. Supervision of wrestlers at all practices and matches

4. Inventory and distribution of equipment and uniforms

5. Media releases (see Figure 9-7)

6. Varsity statistics (see Figure 4-1)

7. Communications with athletic director and principal

8. Check eligibility of all wrestlers

9. Scout opponents (see Figure 5-2)

10. Select and award "Wrestler of the Week" or other honors

11. Check medical kit and work cooperatively with trainer(s)

12. Organize managers and statisticians (see Figure 5-3)

13. Discipline wrestlers when necessary

14. Arrange schedule and necessary transportation

15. Home match preparation

The head coach, in short, leads by example. His commitment, attitude, and effort establish the model assistant coaches and wrestlers should follow. This is an awesome task. A varsity athlete at University High School in Hawaii sums it up well: "An effective coach is someone who knows the game and the competition like the back of his hand. He has to be able to devote his time into coaching and making the team better both in-season an off-season. He has to push athletes to strive to be better and never give up."

A veteran athletic director summarizes: "The head coach will be responsible for the overall management and supervision of their sport program for grades 7–12. Even though the middle school team practices and competes separate from the high school team, they are still part of the total team structure of that particular sport. The head coach should also assign responsibilities and duties to assistant coaches with the approval of the athletic director."

ASSISTANT COACHES

Assistant coaches are the true foundation of any successful program. The head coach cannot do it alone and assistants' commitment to the program is crucial. To get them to commit themselves to your program you should acknowledge their leadership, give them responsibilities, and request their advice, especially regarding match strategies and instructional techniques.

Accepting feedback is important to developing an assistant's motivation and productivity. The head coach should seek input from assistant coaches but be ready to declare the final word in all decisions related to the overall program. Harmony and agreement are important, however, and the feelings and advice of assistants must be considered. "This one part of coaching I like best," says Greg Easter, head wrestling coach at Illinois Valley Central High School. "I enjoy being around the other coaches. I value many of the friendships that have lasted through the years."

Selecting Assistant Coaches

Select assistants based on their . . .

☑ professional credentials;

☑ personal background;

☑ emotional temperament;

☑ desire to work with young athletes;

☑ love for the sport;

☑ technical knowledge;

☑ loyalty and commitment to the head coach and the program;

☑ ability to teach;

☑ integrity and attitude; and

☑ common sense.

Determining Their Responsibilities

When deciding the responsibilities to be given to assistants, consider the knowledge and personality of each one. These responsibilities and duties must be clearly defined, and each should carry its own deadline for completion. Here are ten typical guidelines to follow when assigning tasks:

1. Delegate *meaningful* responsibilities to them.

2. Ask for their advice and input about the program.

3. Have high expectations for them.

4. Have strategy sessions (at least weekly) and remain in constant communication with them.

5. Praise them in public, especially in front of the wrestlers.

6. Never criticize them in public.

7. Support their decisions (especially regarding disciplining wrestlers) in public.

8. Encourage their rapport with wrestlers and parents.

9. Demand their loyalty.

10. Evaluate them fairly and always let them know where they stand (see Figure 5-4 and Figure 5-5).

An assistant coach may be responsible, for instance, for the team's running or weightlifting during the season. You may make him explain the itinerary for an upcoming tournament or teach a special technique. Afterwards, acknowledge that coach's effort for completing that task successfully. Don't expect your assistant coaches to teach or motivate kids like you do. In fact, you should prefer they use their own style and not be your clone.

Assessing Their Commitment

An assessment of your staff should be initiated before the season begins. This can be accomplished through an individual or group discussion:

☑What are their views of the returning wrestlers?

☑What are their objectives? How important is winning to them?

☑How have they dealt with kids in the past?

☑What are they willing to do for the program?

☑What tasks are they most confident about performing?

It is not unreasonable to expect them to perform according to certain standards through the course of the season. They should . . .

☑be enthusiastic and positive during practice;

☑be interested in working with young people;

☑remain loyal to the head coach and the school;

☑be prepared to work extra hours;

☑be cooperative with other members of the coaching staff;

☑enjoy competition; and

☑handle both defeat and victory in a dignified manner.

Each assistant needs to feel important in the overall program, to experience the pleasure of contributing successfully to the team, and to have the opportunity to utilize his talents. Woody Hayes selected his assistants based on their character, personality, work habits, and technical competence. He reasoned that if he found someone tops in the first three, he could teach them whatever else they needed to know.

Dr. Charles M. Shaddow, Principal at Cleveland Heights High School, one of the largest schools in Ohio, looks for more subjective qualities when hiring assistant coaches: "I prefer selecting coaches who have a *passion* for excellence, the ability to *teach,* and *warmth* as a human being."

If you consider using a parent as a volunteer coach, exercise caution. The parent of a wrestler potentially could act in a biased manner to the detriment of everyone concerned.

Assigning Duties to Assistant Coaches

1. Practice instruction

2. Supervise locker room area before and after practice

3. Scout opponents (see Figure 5-2)

4. Arrange for videotaping of competitions and/or practices

5. Assist with medical needs of wrestlers

6. Junior Varsity statistics (see Figure 4-1)

7. Help recruit athletes into the program

8. Attend all wrestling staff meetings and scrimmages

9. Attend booster club meetings

10. Assist with equipment and uniform inventory

11. Act as a referee for wrestle-offs

12. Discipline athletes when necessary

13. Name Junior Varsity Wrestler of the Week

14. Assist with home match preparations

JUNIOR HIGH COACHES—YOUR PIED PIPERS

Select a junior high coach carefully. This person has to have a captivating personality that instills confidence, much like the pied piper in Robert Browning's famous narrative poem whose music drew all the children of Hamelin away from their parents. Like a pied piper, the junior high coach must have a genuine concern for his wrestlers. He also has to stay on top of the techniques of the sport so his team has its best potential for achieving success.

This person has to be popular. He has to be a motivator, respecting the junior high age group and welcoming the position as their coach. The junior high coach needs a special understanding of this age group's needs and maturity level in order to be a positive influence in their lives.

The junior high wrestler has to have faith in this person and know he will always follow through. A solid rapport between coach and team must exist. At the junior high level the program must also be fun so this coach must have a sense of humor.

"I like being a part of his team," says Josh Cook about his middle school coach. He appreciates that his coach "helped me get over my mistakes. He didn't get mad.

He made it fun." A teammate says the coach "gave me confidence. He believes in his athletes and doesn't care if you win or lose."

Typical duties for a junior high coach resemble those of the high school head coach although the head coach should try to lessen his overall work load. The head coach could, for example, arrange the junior high transportation and check those wrestlers' eligibility with the athletic director.

The junior high coach must, however, distribute and collect all necessary forms, maintain his own medical kit, update his kids' statistics weekly, assist in the inventory process, and effectively teach wrestling techniques that continually focus on proper position and basic fundamentals. Junior high wrestlers should graduate into the high school program with a thorough knowledge of federation rules, illegal holds, dangerous positions, improper manuevers, and team policies. They should understand top, bottom, and neutral positions and be prepared to be dynamic competitors who want to "attack" opponents.

Some individuals could see this coaching duty as demeaning or unimportant. Don't allow these types to coach your junior high squad. They could ruin a young wrestler's enthusiasm for the sport. Also, be prepared to dismiss an assistant coach when he fails to follow through with your expectations after several opportunities.

Some coaching staffs have weekly, formal meetings while others may choose to discuss matters occasionally at a favorite restaurant. I suggest you plan at least one meeting each week to discuss the team's past performances and future progress. You choose the site.

To ensure everyone is prepared to contribute effectively at that meeting, present (either orally or in writing) a suggested agenda to them at least two days beforehand. You should also request suggestions and additions to your list before preparing a final agenda. Finally, do not schedule your meeting at an awkward or inconvenient time.

PLANNING SESSIONS THAT KEEP YOU ON TRACK

Key Point #1—"What's on the Agenda Today?"

That is one way to begin, but these meetings should be more focused. The agenda should not be a sporadic discussion of wrestlers or events. Instead, the conversation should usually revolve around personnel, strategy, and techniques. Meetings like this must have a purpose that leads to specific actions. The meeting must end with the coaches ready to transform talk into action. Often, the most logical initial item could be determining the line up.

Key Point #2—"How Effectively Are Our Kids Performing?"

Consider each individual wrestler's status: (1) any injury; (2) skill level; (3) effort at practice or in the recent competition; (4) attitude; (5) talent; and (6) knowledge. Wrestle-offs or challenge matches may have already determined the line-up, but the coaching staff should always have the final word on who competes. An Ohio volleyball coach who has had only one losing season in nearly twenty years of coaching attributes her success to "my staff's ability to accurately judge talent and use that to our advantage. We didn't want to just force players into a system; instead we worked to create a system to complement the players." This approach is beneficial for wrestling, too.

Key Point #3—"What Is the Best Strategy for Our Next Opponent?"

This relates more to dual meets as some opponents may have specific tendencies that you need to prepare to counter. Here, the coaches should devise the methods for teaching wrestlers how to deal with that opponent's special technique (fireman's carry, for instance). The more detailed they are, the better.

The coaches are teachers. They have to know how to communicate the important strategies that help kids win, while understanding the problems that could potentially interfere with the wrestlers accepting and mastering those skills.

Finally, the coaching staff needs to plan activities that correspond effectively with the time allotted to them (usually 1-3 hours), the available facilities and equipment, and the needs of their fellow coaches in the building. Then it is time to put those plans into action. Everyone must be committed to a successful outcome.

Key Point #4—"How Is Your Family Doing?"

Meetings should also reflect the coach's comradery. They can simply be sessions where family events are described or social plans are made. Above all, the members of the coaching staff should be linked by friendship and function as professionals. In this regard, the head coach should work to develop effective relationships among assistants. He should continually evaluate his staff for their interpersonal relationships and attitudes.

Administrators become seriously concerned about a coaching staff, according to Dr. Shaddow, when it has "lost control of the situation and isn't good for the students. Coaches need to remain on an even keel and be good role models. I continually monitor the direction the program is going." Mark Rodgriguez, athletic director at Cuyahoga Community College in Ohio, shares the same concerns. "I know each staff is different, but if the circumstances reveal dishonesty, insubordination, or the general inability to handle the job, then I usually decide to nonrenew them. I think an effective staff is well organized and knows what they want to accomplish and how to accomplish it."

Demand cooperation, if necessary, and offer social skills training to individuals who struggle to get along with others. One way to prevent disagreements during the season is to take a retreat before the season to promote a feeling of cooperation.

Key Point #5—"When Are You Available for Our First Meeting?"

When the wrestling staff meets for the first time before the season actually begins, some typical agenda items should be:

1. to determine a potential roster. The staff must decide who will contact athletes in the school, who will check their grades, and who will distribute/collect necessary forms;

2. to decide what other schools to scrimmage;

3. to organize a practice schedule and a calendar of important events like "Picture Day," "Parents Night," and booster club meetings;

4. to plan any fund raising for tournament meal money or special awards, i.e., Wrestler of the Week;

5. to discuss potential team leaders (captains);

6. to arrange to have matches videotaped;

7. to decide the staff's policies on weight loss, discipline, and post-season awards;

8. to organize the first team meeting with the kids;

9. to establish a plan for dealing with injuries during practice; and

10. to discuss techniques.

Again, avoid any random or "off the cuff" discussions when the coaching staff meets initially to prepare for the upcoming season. By following the agenda above, the coaches can make significant preparations that lead to successful outcomes for both the team and individual wrestlers. Prior to this meeting, the head coach can invite assistants to offer items they feel should be added to the agenda. This invitation increases their stake in the program and heightens their commitment.

RELATIONSHIPS WITH COACHES IN OTHER SPORTS

Establishing a competitive program in any sport would be impossible at Lancaster High School in Ohio, according to coach Tom McCurdy, unless the coaches at his school cooperated and communicated regularly with each other. No one takes private ownership of the athletes. "That's the whole thing, working hand in hand, so you don't schedule football camp the same time you have basketball camp, or you don't schedule open gym at the same time where there's basketball practice."

"Poor relationships with other staff members could result in a coach's nonrenewal," says Joe Giancola, Assistant Superintendent for the Kent City Schools. "The coach has to relate well to other coaches, teachers, principals, and so on. If there is unethical or incompetent behavior in that regard, then a nonrenewal decision could be made."

Clearly, the key is to cooperate effectively with all other school personnel. That way, everyone benefits, especially the athletes. Be sensitive to other coaches' concerns and be an active participant in encouraging positive relationships between all coaching staffs. Compromise may be involved, but if you show a willingness to sacrifice, then your fellow coaches are obligated to do the same. Neglecting relations with other coaches could result in your feeling alienated from them and losing their support.

*"Leadership is the ability to get men to do
what they don't want to do and like doing it."*

—(FROM HARRY TRUMAN)

FIGURE 5-1 DAILY SCHEDULE

TODAY'S PRIORITIES

DATE: _____

Talk to . . .

_____ about _____

_____ about _____

_____ about _____

_____ about _____

_____ about _____

_____ about _____

Take care of . . .   Time

_____ by __ : _____

_____ by __ : _____

_____ by __ : _____

_____ by __ : _____

_____ by __ : _____

_____ by __ : _____

_____ by __ : _____

_____ by __ : _____

Messages Received:

_____ from _____

_____ from _____

_____ from _____

_____ from _____

FIGURE 5-2 SCOUT SHEET

SCOUT SHEET for _____ **HS against** _____ **HS**

WEIGHT CLASS _____ NAME _____

NEUTRAL POSITION

Favorite Set Ups: _____

_____

Takedowns used: _____

_____

Counters used: _____

_____

How can we take him down? _____

_____

_____

TOP

Breakdowns used: _____

_____

Favorite rides:_____

_____

Pinning combo's: _____

_____

Best escape against him?_____

_____

©1996 by Parker Publishing Company

FIGURE 5-2 CONTINUED

<u>BOTTOM</u>

First escape: _____

How can we pin him? _____

_____

FIGURE 5-3 ORGANIZATION OF STATISTICIANS

Guidelines for the Statisticians of _____ High School

I   OBJECTIVES

     A. To promote wrestling at _____ High School

     B. To work at the scoretables at all matches & tournaments

     C. To serve as hostesses at our home tournament

     D. To educate others about the sport of wrestling

     E. To promote school spirit

II   MEMBERSHIP

     A. Membership is open to all students—male and female—in grades 9–12.

     B. Members must pay assigned dues.

     C. Members are obligated to learn the scoring system associated with wrestling before the start of the season.

     D. Any fund raising will be conducted by all members (i.e., selling program advertisements, bake sales).

     E. Officers will be elected at the final meeting and will serve during the following season:

President -	must conduct all meetings, instruct members about the scoring system, and appoint committees as needed
Vice-President -	must conduct meetings in the absence of the president, serve as the chairperson for assigned committees, and assist in teaching the scoring system
Secretary -	must keep the minutes of all meetings and log the progress of all committees
Treasurer -	must account for the club's finances and receive and disburse all funds as needed

III   REQUIREMENTS

     A. Manage scorebook or bout cards at matches and/or tournaments

     B. Make posters and banners for upcoming matches

     C. Assist in the management of all home matches/tournaments

     D. Attend meetings and matches faithfully

     E. Seek sponsors/advertisers for the program and assist in the development of a program or media guide

     F. Provide refreshments (i.e., oranges, sodas) for wrestlers

©1996 by Parker Publishing Company

FIGURE 5-4 ASSISTANT COACH EVALUATION FORM #1

COACHING EVALUATION

This form is to be used to provide a formative and summative evaluation instrument of assistant coaches. The **Narrative Section** should be completed throughout the year, whenever appropriate, as the season progresses in order to provide feedback and encouragement for continued movement toward excellence. The **Coach's Comments Section** provides the assistant coach the opportunity to engage in self-evaluation and to offer his insights about the overall program.

Item #1   The coach cooperated in the management and supervision of the program 7-12.

_____ Satisfactory

_____ Unsatisfactory

_____

Narrative:

_____

Coach's Comments:

_____

Item #2   The Coach conducted himself in a fair, sympathetic, understanding, and positive manner with all athletes which led to their developing a positive self-image and displaying good sportsmanship.

_____ Satisfactory

_____ Unsatisfactory

_____

Narrative:

_____

Coach's Comments:

_____

Item #3   The coach encouraged teamwork, participation, morale, discipline, and competitiveness while considering at all times the overall health and welfare of the athletes.

_____ Satisfactory

_____ Unsatisfactory

FIGURE 5-4 CONTINUED

Narrative: _____

Coach's Comments: _____

Item #4   The coach completed assigned duties and responsibilities in an efficient and punctual manner; attended required meetings; and performed according to the policies and regulations as established by our local school board/ administration and state athletic association.

_____ Satisfactory

_____ Unsatisfactory

Narrative: _____

Coach's Comments: _____

Principal's Signature _____

Head Coach's Signature _____

Asst. Coach's Signature _____

FIGURE 5-5 ASSISTANT COACH EVALUATION FORM #2

ASSISTANT COACH EVALUATION FORM

_____

(NAME)   (DATE)

SCALE: 1. Effective/Satisfactory

2. Needs Improvement/More Training

3. Unsatisfactory/Refer to Comments

4. Not Applicable

Professional Qualifications

_____   1. Cooperates with athletic director and head coach

_____   2. Understands and follows the policies and rules established by the board of education and state athletic association

_____   3. Develops a rapport with entire coaching staff

_____   4. Displays a professional and well-groomed appearance

_____   5. Attends athletic department meetings, awards programs, pep assemblies, etc.

_____   6. Maintains a professional and dignified sideline conduct, especially towards officials, athletes, and opponents

_____   7. Works cooperatively with other assistant coaches and teachers

Coaching Skills

_____   1. Communicates effectively the rules of the sport

_____   2. Uses the appropriate language, behavior, and manners with athletes and parents

_____   3. Provides proper supervision of wrestlers at practice, in the locker room, on the bus, and after a competition

_____   4. Displays a competent knowledge of wrestling

_____   5. Maintains discipline with athletes

FIGURE 5-5 CONTINUED

_____ 6. Accepts the philosophy, policies, and techniques taught by the head coach

_____ 7. Knows CPR, injury policies, and other medical aspects related to wrestling

_____ 8. Is prompt to meetings, practices, and competitions

Personal Characteristics

_____ 1. Remains fair, understanding, and tolerant with athletes and staff

_____ 2. Displays integrity and sincerity

_____ 3. Shows a sincere interest in the wrestlers

_____ 4. Provides positive, confident leadership

_____ 5. Is cooperative and receptive to suggestions from the athletic director and head coach

Comments

_____
(HEAD COACH'S SIGNATURE)   (ASST. COACH'S SIGNATURE)

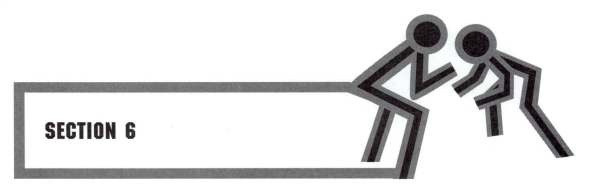

SECTION 6

Successful Practices—The Five W's

"I expect practice to keep me in good shape," says Kent State University wrestler Scott Blank. "That's what gets me ready for competition."

Teammate Joe Boardwine, a two-time state high school wrestling champion, agrees: "My coach has made the difference for me by teaching me a work ethic as well as techniques at practice. I think a coach should be expert on the technical aspects of the sport and also teach the lessons of life."

"I see good practices as an opportunity for the athletes," says Steve Franco, superintendent of the Richmond Heights Schools. "It is their chance to combine the acquisition of knowledge with actual application. Many areas of their skill development are enhanced at practice and contribute to their growth as an athlete and as a person."

Clearly, what happens for wrestlers at practice has a major influence on what happens for them in competitions. Coaches must make their wrestlers recognize the importance of practicing with intensity and diligence. Kids have to be directed to take responsibility for their own success in practice. They can't expect the coaches to do it all.

To get wrestlers to create a successful practice on their own, the coach needs to design practices that begin with clear objectives and involve specific activities. Furthermore, if you can consider practice as a presentation of information (strategies in an underhook/overhook situation, for example) you can devise the structure that empowers kids to master that material.

The coach has to project credibility (*You have mastered the technique and all its variables*) and believability (*The kids are convinced the technique can work for them*). The coach also has to stay in control: he is prepared for potential interruptions, annoying distractions, and unexpected questions especially when he's teaching very technical skills.

At practice, wrestlers should look upon their coach as an expert who knows what they need to do in order to win. This involves detailed organization for each day. The coach accomplishes this by utilizing the five W's of a successful practice: When, Where, What, Who, and Why.

TELL THEM WHEN

As the coach for the Super Bowl champion Oakland Raiders, John Madden operated under two rules: (1) "Be on time" and (2) "Play like hell." The importance of time cannot be underrated by the effective coach. This doesn't refer just to the wrestlers' attendance or punctuality. Effective time management also depends on the coach planning the sequence of step-by-step activities that the team needs to cover. Once he arranges these steps he needs to consider the total time he has to accomplish them and then determine how much time the team can spend on each one. He should follow an organized practice schedule each day (see Figures 6-1, 6-2, and 6-3).

Time Belongs to Everyone

The wrestlers have to know when their practice activities begin, what the sequence will be, the time alloted for each activity, and when practice ends. Time belongs to everyone, not just the coach.

Sometimes, one coach's one-hour practice seems to go on for eternity while another's two-hour practice seems to end too quickly. "Practices are like classes," says Norwalk High School athletic director Mike Grose. "In fact, practices may better prepare the students for their futures than do most classes. The competition and the practicing that take place help develop the student and lead them to success after they are out of school. That's why the coach has to be organized and knowledgable at practice."

The Length of Practice

The length of practice should be determined based on several variables: the age of the wrestlers, their level of maturity, the stage of the season, their knowledge, and their physical condition. Generally, short practices are suitable for the younger (8–12) athlete while longer ones are usually not a problem for the older, better conditioned wrestler.

How much time you need for practice depends also on the kind of skills you need to teach. You should anticipate the questions and difficulties the kids will have prior to the practice and develop an interesting session that gets the wrestlers excited and eager to participate without delays.

Jim Andrassy, another Kent State University varsity wrestler, has been a Mid-American Conference champion and a winner of 106 college matches. For him, practice is valuable time that brings out "the importance of competing, winning, and losing in a good manner. I enjoy the competition and the physical fitness."

TELL THEM WHERE

Athletes must be clear about the facility they will use to perform the activity. Just saying, "Meet in the gym after school" can still leave some wrestlers unprepared for the specific goals of the practice. Where should they begin? At midcourt? The foul lines? The end line (ready for sprinting)?

And what equipment is needed? Running shoes or wrestling shoes? Sweatshirts or t-shirts? Kneepads? Headgears? The kids need this information in advance (the day before is usually suitable). In time, your wrestlers will become familiar with your weekly routine and know where to go and how to dress.

Using Facilities Efficiently

Efficiency is important. Here again, you need to plan in advance for what you want to accomplish. You also need to discuss the use of facilities with other coaches at the school to prevent any interruptions of their practices. The physical environment of your facility (wrestling room) must be considered for its maximum use. Is there enough space for everyone to wrestle matches simultaneously or should you break them up into round-robin groups? Is the weight room nearby or will wrestlers have to travel for several minutes to get to it? Is there room for extended running or should you move them into the school hallways? All these items should be analyzed when planning a practice.

Supervising Effectively

Planning *where* your wrestlers will begin and end practice means arranging for their supervision as well. "When I decide to nonrenew a coach, it's usually because of a lack of supervision," says one principal. "I think coaches need to have an expertise in the field and be a motivator, but they also just need to like communicating and being with kids, not somewhere else."

Supervision cannot be neglected whether before, during, or after practice. As cited in Section 3, coaches risk a liability problem if they fail to supervise their wrestlers properly. When wrestlers are engaged in competitive matches or intense drills in the wrestling room, the coach's presence is especially required. He needs to oversee their movements from one area to the next (wrestling room, gym, locker room) so that they move smoothly and safely.

TELL THEM WHAT

This "W" refers to the actual content of your practice: the warm-up and conditioning; the activities and techniques, the exercises and skills.

Determining Training Methods and Practice Activities

Involve the wrestlers themselves in the actual teaching process and begin technique instruction by briefly discussing with wrestlers their opinions about the techniques you plan to cover:

"How would you finish from here?"

"Why is this an effective set up?"

"What am I doing wrong here, why can't I complete my stand up?"

This type of dialogue can often eliminate confusion about the purpose or skill related to a specific move. Question and answer sessions help wrestlers improve their thinking skills and provide the coach with an indication of how well he has taught the technique. Of course, when demonstrating techniques or strategies, the coach has several options:

1. he can demonstrate the technique;

2. a highly-skilled wrestler can demonstrate;

3. video or film can be used;

4. pictures and illustrations can be used; and/or

5. lecture and describe it.

Coaches should provide various demonstrations of important techniques (often from different angles) and possibly relate the new manuever to some previously-mastered skill. A continuous dialogue between coach and wrestlers should take place while moves are taught. Here, the coach can discover who can add to the explanation and who may not understand it. This keeps wrestlers active during instruction, not passive observers.

Clarity is crucial. In fact, the more simplistic the explanation the better the kids will understand. Maintain eye contact with the team as much as possible, raise and lower the volume of your voice, and speak in a conversational tone. All this will keep your wrestlers' attention and help them understand.

For most athletes the best teacher is repetition. They learn best when the coach teaches moves by (1) explaining the technique or strategy, (2) demonstrating it, (3) observing the wrestlers drill it, and (4) having them repeat the correct technique to gain mastery. Just find different ways to repeat the same thing.

More repetition may be needed for some wrestlers, and individual tutoring is often helpful. Your patience during this instructional process is necessary. Don't be afraid to criticize, but work to solve the problem, not create another one.

It is also clear that today's coaches should employ far more sophisticated training methods than were needed ten years ago. If the skills of the sport can become instinctive for a wrestler, he can perform more quickly and successfully in a competition. Experienced coaches know that the sport of wrestling is based on habit and repetition. You can't compete one way in practice and another way in a match. It's a reflex. Quick actions are required, and wrestlers often don't have time to think.

There are some important keys to teaching at practice the methods and skills associated with wrestling:

1. Make the activity directly related to match situations.

2. Make sure the wrestlers can accomplish the activity, that it relates appropriately to their age and skill-level.

3. Allow enough time to accomplish the activity.

4. Change the activity if the wrestlers become sluggish or unenthused; a variety of challenging drills is best.

5. Be sure the wrestlers are clear about the objective of the activity.

6. Demand that kids stay quiet during any instruction or match situation.

7. Begin skill practice slowly and then pick up the speed.

"Practice without improvement is meaningless."

—(FROM CHUCK KNOX, AN NFL COACH)

How you begin practice has a major influence on how athletes perform in practice that day. A brief meeting where you explain that practice's routine and schedule is useful, or you can demand that the wrestlers initiate their warm-up routine as soon as they step on the mat. A sample warm-up is provided in Section 7.

The coach needs to determine a specific sequence of steps that can take the wrestler from his present skill level to a more advanced level. As the wrestler works at each step, there should be a high probability that he can master it. The steps shouldn't be too large or complex (they should be easy to understand and perform). Of course, the coach should provide constant reinforcement or rewards after each attempt.

Creating an Environment for Success

Make practice sessions active for your wrestlers. Their learning should be an active, not a passive process. Everyone should be involved at every moment whether they're doing takedown drills or peer coaching.

Sometimes, you can have your wrestlers begin by practicing their own individual techniques or specialties after they have warmed up. When athletes are self-directed like this (while under your observation), you can provide more individualized instruction and correct their mistakes. This also can enable them to take some element of control over their own skill development and improvement as a wrestler.

*"Repeated actions are stored as habits.
If the repeated actions aren't funda-
mentally sound, then what comes out in
a game can't be sound. What comes out
will be bad habits."*

—(FROM CHUCK KNOX, NFL COACH)

Through the course of the practice, the coach should be cautious about fatigue. Heavy training sessions shouldn't be coupled with learning new skills. "An effective coach," says Larry Hoon, who has been a head wrestling coach for 23 years, "runs an organized and efficient practice and simply has a plan for success. I'm also not afraid to venture beyond the teaching of moves or techniques and spend time getting to be friends with my kids."

*"All forms of athletics require highly skilled
endeavors. To accomplish such skills, only
concentrated practice helps toward perfection.
Practice without concentration or without
knowledge of what you're doing is worthless."*

—(FROM ANDY VARIPAPA, PROFESSIONAL BOWLER)

You should avoid introducing new techniques late in the week or late in the season, since this could prompt anxiety in some wrestlers who then won't learn what you're trying to teach.

The coach should demand that athletes practice both physical and mental skills. "Nobody ever mastered any skill," says Norman Vincent Peale, "except through intensive, persistent, and intelligent practice. Practice it the right way." Their physical effort may require a lot of sweat; their mental effort requires constant concentration. Wrestlers can be taught to mentally review technique and perform a sequence of drills in their minds' eye.

The drudgery of practice. Olympic coach "Doc" Counsilman used silly antics and obnoxious humor to make his swimming practices fun. Coaches must try to make practice an enjoyable experience but not a party. A varsity wrestler adds: "Practice has to be fun. I want practice to raise my level of competition, but I also expect the coach to give all athletes an equal chance and help all the athletes in the same way." Be sure, therefore, to add fun into the learning process. While repetition is needed in drills, learning need not be boring or dull. Consider that hardship in practice doesn't necessarily translate into winning matches.

Keep learning. The coaches should be students of their sport themselves. Updated textbooks, coaching clinics, top-notch videotapes, and effective dialoging with other coaches can improve coaches' understanding of wrestling. According to Richard Greene, principal of Chillicothe Elementary Center in Illinois, the coach has to keep learning. "The coach must first possess a thorough knowledge of the sport and be able to communicate that knowledge well. If I have to fire a coach it's usually because he or she is abusive, poorly organized, or poorly prepared in the knowledge of the game."

Teaching excellence is still the common denominator. Successful teachers and successful coaches share the same principles and attributes.

TELL THEM WHO (THE BUDDY SYSTEM)

Here is excellent advice for coaches who want practice to be a successful and rewarding experience for their wrestlers: Recent research has shown that when a peer teaches another wrestler he learns at a faster rate than when instructed under normal coach/wrestler circumstances.

Teaching Cooperation

Therefore, it is wise to form pairs of wrestlers at the first practice of the season—older athletes (seniors and juniors) with younger ones (sophomores and freshmen). This helped Nick Lisco as a varsity wrestler for St. Edwards High School improve as an athlete and become a state tournament place finisher. "I was always pushed to do my best, win or lose. I also enjoyed the competition and the hard workouts."

This format works especially well for drilling, but the wrestlers must be willing to work together. Drill partners must be open-minded and willing to listen to each other. They also have to put forth 100 percent effort. Intensity is a strong part of drilling if it is to be effective. Both must share the same commitment level and attitude regarding mastering techniques and being successful. Both must be willing to make a strong contribution to the other's achievement.

Drill partners should know to give minimum resistance at the beginning stages of drilling a manuever and increased resistance through the repeated execution of that skill. This enables both wrestlers to gain confidence in mastering the technique and in each other.

Making Wrestlers Responsible for Their Own Achievement

Before the coach pairs up the members of his team, he should study their attitudes and goals. Drill partners should be mutually supportive—encouraging each other's improvement, enhancing each other's skills, and maximizing each other's conditioning.

Having wrestlers work with the same partner like this on a daily basis can contribute equally to each athlete's psychological and physical development. Their attention span and self-discipline improve when they are responsible to a specific teammate. Anxiety and other emotions are often lessened when these burdens can be shared with a partner. If they are paired correctly, each wrestler shares the same goals and objectives as his counterpart, which can enhance their mental preparation for upcoming competitions.

If each wrestler views his partner's training as importantly as his own, then both perform better in practice and in matches. Furthermore, both are more likely to recover from poor performances more quickly. The coach should observe his wrestlers, through the buddy system, get in better condition and communicate more openly with their peers. In short, team building occurs.

TELL THEM WHY

Reasons and Responsibility

Be sure that the wrestlers recognize the reasons for each activity at practice. They have to grasp the concept behind the skill as well as the results you're aiming for. Most often, a quick explanation—"You need to do it this way because . . ." or "Here's why it's important to do it this way"—can accomplish this.

When they accept the reasons, wrestlers are more willing to take on the responsibility for mastering a technique, for overcoming their limitations, and for reshaping their skills. An ultimate outcome is for them to take on the responsibility for their own success and/or defeat in competition.

The wrestlers who accept this kind of responsibility come to see instruction as an opportunity to eliminate a weakness and improve performance. After recognizing the importance of mastering a certain skill, they are eager to test themselves at it even if it isn't easily accomplished. They show more effort and listen more closely. They are also more under control.

The wise coach, therefore, prefaces instruction and commands by first listing the reasons that make learning any skill necessary. He then provokes the wrestlers' sense of ambition by challenging them to persevere beyond their initial mistakes. Finally, he adds to the challenge by adding onto it (another finish to a takedown, for example) until he is convinced their mental and physical energy is focused on mastering the maneuver and surpassing their limitations. To accomplish this, part of an effective practice is having a disciplined approach.

The Purpose of Practice

Practice has to be purposeful, and the wrestlers need to know what is expected of them. They should expect, in fact, to come ready to learn. One varsity wrestler acknowledges that practice "taught me how to diet properly, how to wrestle better, how to condition on my own, and how to be committed. The best coach for me is someone who can teach you the right way to do something, rather than letting you continue to do the wrong thing."

Here are ten important keys to making practice an enjoyable and rewarding experience for your wrestlers:

1. Keep them busy.

2. Reward dutiful attendance.

3. Vary the practice schedule.

4. Surprise them occasionally.

5. Allow them to give input about the practice schedule or have the better-skilled wrestlers teach techniques to the less-skilled athletes.

6. Allow for individual instruction on a daily basis.

7. Use competitive (sometimes game-oriented) drills.

8. Provide extrinsic rewards for diligent practice habits (a t-shirt, patch, or certificate).

9. Shorten practices especially in the season's final weeks.

10. Give your wrestlers a day off (go to a movie together, have a pizza party, whatever).

A final recommendation is to be flexible. On some days you may discover that the team is troubled or concerned about some school or social issue. It's interfering with their concentration on the tasks you've planned for practice, and they're sluggish through every drill. Be ready, therefore, to talk about it and make adjustments.

THE PRACTICE SCHEDULE

Each Month

A basic and obvious objective here is to prepare your wrestlers for meet and tournament competition. The first two months in the season involve more learning and drilling during practice time while your final months require more competitive wrestling to help the squad peak for the tournaments.

You could follow the format below, which serves as a guide for instruction organized on a month-to-month basis for a typical two-and-a-half-hour daily practice:

November—December

Priority: Emphasis on Orientation, Instruction, and Mastery

A.   Warm-up and Agility and Power Drills   20 min.

B.	Running	20 min.
C.	Weightlifting (2-3 times a week)	25 min.
D.	Instruction	35 min.
E.	Drilling	35 min.
F.	Competitive Wrestling	15 min.

January

Priority: Emphasis on Improvement, Conditioning, and Fun

A.	Warm-up and Agility and Power Drills	20 min.
B.	Running	10 min.
C.	Weightlifting (2 times a week)	20 min.
D.	Instruction	25 min.
E.	Drilling	25 min.
F.	Competitive Wrestling	45-50 min.

February—March

Priority: Emphasis on Achieving Goals and Peaking

A.	Warm-up and Agility and Power Drills	15 min.
B.	Running	10 min.
C.	Weightlifting (1-2 times a week)	20 min.
D.	Instruction	15 min.
E.	Drilling	20 min.
F.	Competitive Wrestling	50 min.

Each Week

More detailed organization is required here. Specific skills and techniques need to be placed in a day-to-day sequence that results in the wrestlers mastering them. Select skills to teach from each of the basic positions in wrestling—neutral, top, and bottom. Don't be afraid to specialize (for example, I like leg rides on top and seldom teach arm bars). Decide, for instance, if you prefer your team to concentrate on leg attacks or counters from the neutral position and then plan practices accordingly.

You should also review mistakes observed during the previous match or practice and re-emphasize the team goals (see Figure 6-4). You could also plan to announce a "Wrestler of the Week" award for the individual who performed with the highest skill during the week.

Here is a week-by-week progression for the first three weeks of the season:

<u>Week #1</u>

Important Concepts

1. How to drill (the buddy system)
2. Training for mastery/Training to win
3. Avoiding illegal holds and techniques
4. Make the first move and set the match pace
5. Practice rules and training rules
6. Team work and team goals
7. Act vs. React

Agility Drills

<u>Low Level</u>	<u>Advanced Level</u>
1. Forward roll	Dive into forward roll
2. Backward roll	Backward extensions
3. Crab walk to bear walk	Hip heisting
4. Lateral shuffle	Position drill
5. Duck walks	Lower level drill
6. Spin drill	"Float" drill

Technique Instruction

1. Stance and motion
2. Stance, motion, set-up, and penetration—attacking on contact, no "soft" hands
3. Outside single leg attack (high crotch) and finishes
4. Neutral, top, bottom alignments
5. Inside leg stand up
6. Breakdowns and pressure from the top position

<u>Week #2</u>

Important Concepts

1. Knowing when to attack and when not to
2. Moving in a series
3. "Kick him out"—score to win
4. Mat awareness
5. Weight control
6. Conditioning

7.   Selecting alignment and other rules

Agility Drills

	Low Level	Advanced Level
1.	"Froggy"	Wrist control and pressure
2.	Sprawl from knees	Hip down drill
3.	Position drill	Fight the underhook
4.	Bridging	Bridge to hip heist
5.	Lower level drill	Lower level vs. tie up

Technique Instruction

1.   Review stance, motion, set ups, level change, and penetration

2.   Review outside single and finishes

3.   Inside single leg attack and finishes

4.   Counters to leg attacks: sprawl, wizzer, crossface, lines of defense, snap and spin, front headlock

5.   Review inside leg stand up and hand control

6.   Riding and pinning (half nelson and reverse nelson)

Week #3

Important Concepts

1.   Never chase an opponent in the neutral position

2.   Attacking low and high stance

3.   Underhooks and overhooks

4.   Review team goals and improvement

5.   Evaluate conditioning

6.   Scrimmages and first competition

Agility Drills

	Low Level	Advanced Level
1.	Sprawling	Butt drag
2.	Penetration step	Shot/re-shot drill
3.	Hip heist	Hip heist after elevation

Technique Instruction

1.   Review stance, motion, set ups (overhooks and underhooks), penetration

2.   How to come out of a bad shot

3.   Review inside/outside single

4.   Double leg attack

5.   Review wizzer series and front headlock

6.   Riding with the legs—pinning

7.   Stopping opponent's stand up

8.   Improve inside leg stand up

This is a general schedule for the first three weeks of the high school season. By the end of the third week wrestlers have mastered three different leg attacks and two counters from the neutral position, 4-5 breakdowns and two ways to ride from the top position, and the inside leg stand up from the bottom position. They know how to train effectively with a drill partner and to get in top condition. They've drilled proper position, practiced various set ups, and learned offensive and defensive manuevers from all situations on the mat. They understand the importance of aggressive wrestling, moving in a series, and positioning themselves in advantageous alignments. Their weight loss is under control, their attitude is positive, and their team goals are affirmed. In short, they are very ready for their first interscholastic match.

You may choose to proceed at a faster or slower rate and, in fact, teach different techniques. You should note that I favor the repetition of certain techniques; I find that teaching a few moves thoroughly is better than covering many moves briefly. After the third week and the first match, the coaching staff evaluates our strengths and weaknesses and then plans the following weeks' practices to deal with those areas that require improvement.

Each Day

Like the season overall, each practice must have a goal, an objective the coaching staff mandates beforehand that the team has to accomplish. That goal has to be addressed with the team. By the end of practice, that goal should be achieved. Dan Gable recommends that in "every practice session you need to emphasize the areas that give you trouble and drill in those areas. It is important that you feel some self-satisfaction after every practice."

Accomplishment and closure are two keys to any successful practice. The kids must see each practice as a challenge to improve their skills and as another step toward success. They should sense by the end of each practice that they have met that day's challenge and taken that step. They should recognize their work that day is completed, leaving them confident about their skills and eager for the next practice session.

Each practice is itself a competition. Our wrestlers compete to achieve the quality performance we coaches expect of them. Practices should be designed to empower them to experience achievement, allowing for mistakes, corrections, improvement, and finally success.

It is also wise to vary the format and intensity of each practice to prevent boredom or burnout. Although they may coach one group at a competition, all coaches should circulate around the practice room and work with all wrestlers—freshmen, junior varsity, and varsity. This enables each wrestler to receive a lot of feedback on his skills and make greater improvements.

Utilize managers effectively during each practice, too. They can perform administrative duties that free coaches to work more closely with individual wrestlers. Managers are important members of the team and contribute much to the smooth operation of any typical practice. They do, however, need to be monitored and given guidelines (see Figure 6-5).

"You can't get much done in life if you only work on the days when you feel good," Jerry West, an NBA coach, comments, and this message must be transmitted to your wrestlers. Indeed, improvement happens slowly if attendance at each practice becomes a problem. Kids reach their potential faster when they are challenged by the coaches, when they are pushed by their drill partner, and when their talents are stretched at practice each day.

HOW TO DEAL WITH AN INJURED WRESTLER

Although a wrestler may be injured he need not sit out a practice session. He can still work on his skills and rehabilitate his injury in order to remain a competitive member of the team. Rest and recovery are certainly important, but his skills could lessen if he doesn't maintain conditioning and competency. Below are the activities a coach can have injured wrestlers perform during a typical practice.

If his ankle or knee is injured, have him perform the following drills centered on the word four (or forty) for easy recall:

1. Forty situps

2. Forty pushups

3. Four sets of the military bench press

4. Four sets dumbbell lateral raises

5. Four sets of chin ups

5. Four sets of dumbbell curls

6. Four sets of rope climbs

7. Drill with a partner any pinning series

8. Practice half-nelson vs. a partner who tries rolling

9. Snap and spin drill from knees

10. Watch technique video

If his elbow, arm, or shoulder is injured, have him perform these drills, again based on the numeral four:

1. Four sets of shuffle drills against wall, in a circle, and against a partner

2. Four sets of duck walks on mat perimeter

3. Four sets of penetration steps vs. wall, then partner

4. Fourteen minutes of stance and motion drill

5. Fourteen minutes of fix position drills (from knees, from belly)

6. Four sets of squat jumps

7. Forty situps

8. Forty stand ups (20 against wall, 20 against partner)

9. Forty laps on mat perimeter or gym

10. Watch technique video

Unless the wrestler is seriously injured he can still find practice to be a beneficial experience. His teammates won't resent his being inactive, and he can still feel challenged even though he has an injury. However, be cautious of the athlete who may try to do too much and further aggravate his injury. Proper supervision is crucial in these situations.

Coaches must work to link achievement to practice as closely as they do to competitions. Successful practices leave everyone exhausted, yet satisfied with the way the team is progressing. This happens when you organize effectively and communicate this plan concisely, engaging wrestlers in a series of activities that improve their skills, strength, and stamina.

Practice involves a continuous communication between coaches and wrestlers, and everybody, even injured wrestlers, are actively involved in accomplishing the goals for that day or week. If the upcoming competition can be seen as a test (the state tournament would be the final exam), then practice can be likened to classroom work. That makes you the teacher—a teacher who wants each wrestler's performance to earn him an A+.

FIGURE 6-1 EXAMPLE PRACTICE PLAN #1

_____ High School Daily Practice Schedule   Date _____

Time   *Activity*

____   Announcements: _____
                _____

____   Running: _____ Weightlifting: _____

____   Warm-up & Flexibility Drills

____   Daily Drills

                Neutral _____

                Top _____

                Bottom _____

                Instruction—Review

____   Takedowns _____

____   Counters _____

____   Breakdowns _____

____   Rides _____

____   Pins _____

____   Escapes _____

____   Special _____

                Instruction—New

____   Takedowns _____

____   Counters _____

____   Breakdowns _____

____   Rides _____

____   Pins _____

FIGURE 6-1 CONTINUED

_____ Escapes _____

_____ Special _____

Situation Wrestling

_____ 1. _____ Number _____

_____ 2. _____ Number _____

_____ 3. _____ Number _____

_____ 4. _____ Number _____

Competitive Wrestling

_____ 1. _____ Number _____

_____ 2. _____ Number _____

_____ 3. _____ Number _____

_____ 4. _____ Number _____

Conditioning Drills

_____ 1. _____ Number _____

_____ 2. _____ Number _____

_____ Warm-Down _____

FIGURE 6-2 EXAMPLE PRACTICE PLAN #2

_____ High School Daily Practice Schedule   Date _____

TIME	ACTIVITY	ITS PURPOSE
_____	Announcements: _____	
	_____	
_____	Running: _____	_____
_____	Weightlifting: _____	_____
_____	Warm-up & Flexibility Drills	
_____	I AGILITIES	
	_____	_____
	_____	_____
	_____	_____
	_____	_____
_____	II TAKEDOWNS	
	_____	_____
	_____	_____
	_____	_____
	_____	_____
_____	III TOP TECHNIQUES	
	_____	_____
	_____	_____
	_____	_____
	_____	_____
_____	IV BOTTOM TECHNIQUES	
	_____	_____
	_____	_____
	_____	_____
	_____	_____

FIGURE 6-2 CONTINUED

_____   V   COMPETITIVE WRESTLING

Type _____ Time _____ Number _____

Type _____ Time _____ Number _____

Type _____ Time _____ Number _____

Type _____ Time _____ Number _____

Type _____ Time _____ Number _____

Type _____ Time _____ Number _____

_____   VI   CONDITIONING AND WARM DOWN

Type _____ Time _____ Number _____

Type _____ Time _____ Number _____

Type _____ Time _____ Number _____

Type _____ Time _____ Number _____

_____   VII   REMINDERS

_____

_____

FIGURE 6-3 EXAMPLE PRACTICE PLAN #3

_____ DAILY WRESTLING PRACTICE SCHEDULE

DATE _____

TIME ACTIVITY

_____   1.   TEAM MEETING: _____
                   _____

_____   2.   RUNNING _____

_____   3.   WARM-UP & FLEXIBILITY

                   TODAY'S GOAL:_____

_____   4.   WEIGHTLIFTING _____ ROPE CLIMBS _____

             5.   DRILLS / TECHNIQUES

_____   _____

_____   _____

_____   _____

_____   _____

_____   _____

_____   _____

_____   _____

_____   _____

_____   _____

_____   _____

_____   _____

_____   _____

_____   _____

_____   6.   CONDITIONING: _____

FIGURE 6-4 WRESTLING SKILLS REVIEW

_____ PRACTICE REVIEW

DATE _____

Today's outstanding wrestler:_____

Quote for the day: _____

_____

_____

_____

_____

Techniques mastered: _____

_____

_____

_____

_____

Techniques needing improvement: _____

_____

_____

_____

_____

Injuries: _____

_____

_____

Special events today: _____

_____

_____

FIGURE 6-5 INSTRUCTIONS AND GUIDELINES FOR WRESTLING MANAGERS

GUIDELINES FOR WRESTLING MANAGERS

RULES

1. Attend all assigned practices.

2. Attend all scheduled scrimmages and competitions.

3. Never leave the wrestling room or area without receiving permission from a coach.

4. Dress appropriately for practice and competitions.

5. Behave in an appropriate and polite manner during any practice, scrimmage, or competition.

DUTIES

1. Management and inventory of the medical kit and supplies

2. Time all wrestling matches and drill sessions during each wrestling practice. Take responsibility for blowing the whistle at selected intervals.

3. Prepare and fill ice jug before each practice and match.

4. Assist in the set up before each home meet.

5. Design and update wrestling display case.

6. Post statistics and news articles on wrestling bulletin board.

7. Assist coaches during wrestle-offs.

8. Run errands as needed (i.e., deliver forms to administration office).

9. Distribute and/or collect forms from wrestlers.

10. Assist coaching staff in any other duties related to the successful daily operation of the wrestling team.

FIGURE 6-6 OPTIONS FOR RUNNING

1. Outside distance running (2-6 miles).

2. Outside distance running—A team race with "Team A" consisting of the boys in weight classes 103, 119, 130, 140, 152, 171, and 215; and "Team B" consisting of the wrestlers in the weight classes 112, 125, 135, 145, 160, 189, and HWT.

3. Bleacher steps (in your football stadium or gym).

4. Relay races—Sprints, bear runs, crab walks, duck walks—Be sure that groups are small (2-4 wrestlers) to minimize standing around and resting.

5. Laps in the gym or around the perimeter of the mat. You can vary this by having them sprint, jog, and walk on a coach's command (blowing a whistle) to simulate the sudden explosiveness required in a wrestling match.

6. "Indian race"—As the wrestlers run in a single-file line, the last man in line sprints to the front and then sets the pace until the next man sprints to the front. You can also have them pass a ball down the line and when it is handed to the final man he begins his sprint to the front of the line.

7. "Four Corner Sprints"—In the gym or wrestling room, the wrestlers sprint the perimeter's long distance and jog the short distances.

8. Run laps in the gym or wrestling room and have them do either five pushups or five situps in every corner.

9. Timed sprints (i.e., ten seconds to sprint a certain distance).

10. "Hill runs"—Find a steep hill approximately 50-100 yards long and have the wrestlers run it alone 10-20 times.

11. Partner carries around the mat or gym perimeter, switching off only when the coach signals it.

12. Run a match (or two matches) and then an overtime.

13. Line sprints—Do these in the gym or on a wrestling mat where lines are clearly visible. Wrestlers sprint to the line, bend at the knees to touch it, and then sprint back.

14. "Carry the Group"—In a group of four, each wrestler must carry the other members one at a time on his back to a spot designated by the coach (usually the other side of the mat). Each wrestler must carry each member once, sprinting the entire way, deposit him at the designated spot, and then sprint back to get the next member.

©1996 by Parker Publishing Company

FIGURE 6-7 OPTIONS FOR COMPETITIVE WRESTLING

Variations for Competitive Wrestling at Practice

1. Matches

    Engage wrestlers in 4-10 matches per practice, giving them short breaks in between. Be sure they pair up with a different partner at least once.

2. Groups

    You can set up groups of 3, 4, 5, or 6 based on the following sequence of wrestling:

    Group of 3—   1 vs. 2, 3 rests; 1 vs. 3, 2 rests; 2 vs. 3

    Group of 4—   1 vs. 2, 3 vs. 4; 1 vs. 3, 2 vs. 4; 1 vs 4, 2 vs. 3

    Group of 5—   1 vs. 2, 3 vs. 4, 5 rests; 1 vs. 5, 2 vs. 3, 4 rests; 1 vs. 4, 2 vs. 5, 3 rests; 1 vs. 3, 4 vs. 5, 2 rests; 2 vs. 4, 3 vs. 5, 1 rests.

    Group of 6—   1 vs. 2, 3 vs. 4, 5 vs. 6; 1 vs. 5, 2 vs. 3, 4 vs. 6; 1 vs. 4, 2 vs. 5, 3 vs. 6; 1 vs. 3, 4 vs. 5, 2 vs. 6; 2 vs. 4, 3 vs. 5, 1 vs. 6.

3. Situation Wrestling

    Place wrestlers in specific situations—for example, a stalled single leg attack vs. a wizzer. One man must try to finish his attack while the other must counter.

4. Drill Matches

    Here, wrestlers compete against each other using only 80 percent resistance, but moving and drilling at a hurried pace over a specific length of time (2 minutes).

5. Minute Matches

    Compete against the same partner for eleven minutes, allowing each other one one minute break over that time span if they desire.

6. Counter Wrestling

    Begin in the neutral position where one man is only allowed to attempt leg attacks and the other man is only allowed to counter those attacks.

FIGURE 6-7 CONTINUED

7. Free-style and/or Greco-Roman Wrestling

    For a change of pace near the end of the season, have matches where they wrestle one of the Olympic sports. Shift back and forth between collegiate wrestling and one of these types.

8. Shark Bait

    Put the wrestlers in groups and begin with the varsity man in the middle. His fellow group members then rotate in on him for 15-30 seconds each period.

9. "Kick Him Out"

    In pairs, wrestlers begin every time in the optional starting position, alternating themselves after each whistle.

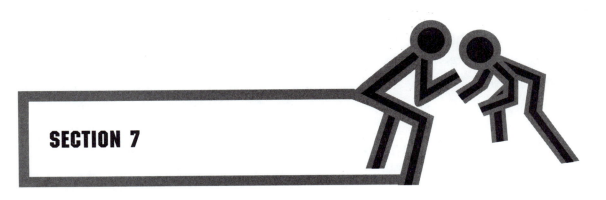

SECTION 7

Skills and Drills

This chapter focuses on the fundamental skills every wrestler should learn in order to avoid position mistakes. Violating proper position from either the neutral, top, or bottom alignments is common among younger wrestlers, so it is crucial they work diligently when performing these drills. Repetition is also important. Your wrestlers are more likely to master a skill if they are directed to repeat it daily.

The format of this chapter is to list the exercise, skill, or drill and explain its purpose (why it is important to achievement in a wrestling competition). The wrestlers should be told this purpose before beginning the activity.

Teach offensive wrestling: As an overview, during all instruction there should be an emphasis on wrestlers having an "attack" attitude, (i.e., they constantly pressure their opponents and always look to score from every position). Defensive wrestling, though important to learn, often leads to dull matches and bored fans. Offensive wrestling, however, is fun to teach and exciting to watch.

You need to make clear to your wrestlers that practice must be an active experience. They must be ready each day to hustle throughout the practice and to wrestle with intensity. Even the stars have much to learn. They can't be permitted to coast on their reputations or slack off. Everyone, including the coach, must give it his best shot.

And it all begins with the warm-up.

WARM-UP AND FLEXIBILITY

Before any intense physical activity begins, the wrestlers' muscles need to be stretched, their hearts have to get pumping, and their minds have to start focusing. A detailed warm-up accomplishes all three.

Good flexibility increases the wrestler's ability to avoid injury and to move more freely in all directions. It also makes him more effective in any "scramble" situation in a match. In short, significant time spent warming up can make the difference between health and harm on the mat.

Here are some general guidelines for an effective warm-up/flexibility routine:

☑Stretch slowly.

☑Avoid bouncing—this ballistic stretching can cause injury and actually tighten muscles.

☑Hold each position 10-20 seconds, going from a mild stretch to a more extended stretch (without pain).

☑Stretching should not generate pain.

☑Tight muscles can cause injuries and affect performance.

☑Concentrate on the muscle being stretched.

Wrestlers should keep these guidelines in mind as they do the following 20 exercises for a basic warm-up.

Activity

1. Jogging in a circle

2. Jog and skip

3. Jog and swing arms

4. Shuffle in/out

Purpose

This succession of activities immediately causes an increased heart rate and prompts blood to flow to all muscle groups. The muscles also go through an effective transition from an inactive status to an active one.

Activity

5. Cartwheels

6. Forward rolls

7. Backward rolls/extensions

Purpose

This stage of the warm-up also increases energy levels and improves endurance. It also assists in increasing the flexibility of the shoulders while loosening up the joints and muscles in the arms. These activities also add to mat awareness.

Activity

8. "Drag the laces" (see Photo 7-1)

PHOTO 7-1

Purpose

The joints in the ankles and knees are flexed, and the muscles in the groin and legs are stretched effectively.

After the intial jogging phase of the warm-up, the team forms a circle with the captain(s) in the center. Each exercise is announced by the captain who then leads the others through the stretch. Example:

Captain:	"Butterflies . . . Ready?"
Team:	"Yes sir!"
Captain:	"Begin!"
Team:	"One."
Captain:	"Two."
Team:	"Three."
Etc.	

This type of dialogue, where the captain and team alternate numbers, not only sets a serious tone to the warm-up (lending credibility, therefore, to its importance), it also makes all athletes mentally active during the stretch. They remain focused on the stretch and create a sense of team unity.

Activity—Standing

9. Groin stretch (see Photo 7-2)

10. Lunges (see Photo 7-3)

11. "Prisoners" (see Photo 7-4)

12. Trunk Twists

Purpose

These exercises help to increase an athlete's range of motion in the joints located in the hips, knees, and ankles.

PHOTO 7-2: Sitting with legs straight, wrestlers spread their legs, then reach to the left, middle, and right, bringing the chest to the mat.

PHOTO 7-3: Standing with legs apart, the wrestlers alternate stepping each foot forward and bending over that knee.

PHOTO 7-4: Wrestlers stand and reach for the ceiling, lifting themselves onto the balls of their feet.

Activity—Sitting

13. Butterflies
14. Back up (see Photo 7-5)
15. Bridging
16. Push ups

Purpose

Here, wrestlers work to increase their range of motion in the joints located in the hips, shoulders, and neck while adding to the stamina of the muscles in these areas. Any tension in these muscle groups is lessened.

PHOTO 7-5: Wrestlers begin with their chests, pelvic area, and legs flat on the mat, then push up and arch their backs, keeping their pelvic area and legs flat.

AGILITY DRILLS

Wrestlers should now join their drill partners and work together on the following agility drills:

Activity—Partners

17. Squats (see Photos 7-6 & 7-7)

Purpose

Wrestlers can strengthen the joints and muscles located in in the hips, legs, and back.

PHOTO 7-6

PHOTO 7-7

Note that wrestlers must maintain a good stance as they squat with their partner on their back.

Activity

18. Lifts (see Photos 7-8 & 7-9)

Purpose

Wrestlers strengthen the joints and muscles located in the shoulders, hips, knees, and arms. This exercise also duplicates the skills required for finishing a high crotch takedown.

PHOTO 7-8

PHOTO 7-9

Note how the wrestlers who are lifting bring their hips in tight to their partner while maintaining control with one arm around the waist and the other around the leg (thigh).

Activity

19. Inverted pushups (see Photo 7-10)

PHOTO 7-10

Purpose

This is a primary strength builder for the arms and shoulders and enables wrestlers to add power to any takedown technique.

Activity

20. Hop Overs (see Photos 7-11—7-16)

Purpose

These increase leg strength while adding flexibility to the joints located in the ankles and knees. This also leads into wrestlers recognizing the importance of power and speed to completing takedown techniques.

PHOTO 7-11

PHOTO 7-12

PHOTO 7-13

PHOTO 7-14

PHOTO 7-15

PHOTO 7-16

Through the course of this drill the bottom wrestler shifts his position from a prone position to a base position, which makes the drill more challenging and increases the stamina of the legs. Note that the hopping wrestlers must maintain a proper stance throughout the drill.

This completes the basic warm-up. Although there is no set time limit, its usual duration is 10-20 minutes (Ten minutes is the minimum adequate time allotment for effective stretching). Some individuals could require more time to improve their flexibility, so don't approach your warm-up session with a "Let's hurry up and get it over with" attitude.

The warm-up period could also serve as a beneficial time to make announcements or to establish goals for that practice. Flex their minds as well as their bodies. At the end they should be stretched, sweating, and prepared.

"You are never better than anyone else until you do something to prove it, and, when you are really good, you never need to tell anyone. They will tell you."

—(FROM KEN VENTURI, SPORTS BROADCASTER)

DRILLS FOR THE NEUTRAL POSITION—OFFENSE

Wrestlers have to be encouraged to be offensive, to push their opponents, and to attack from all directions. In the neutral position, they should move in short, choppy steps and attack only after gaining contact. Fast hands plus fast feet usually equal success in gaining takedowns.

Proper position, of course, is the key. The repetition of the following fundamental drills can help wrestlers identify proper position and regain it when they are caught out of position as typified by the wrestlers in the following photographs (see Photos 7-17—7-19).

PHOTO 7-17

PHOTO 7-18

PHOTO 7-19

Activity

1. Fix Position Drills

   –from one knee

   –from tripod

Purpose

These drills teach wrestlers how to recover from poor positions after attempting a leg attack—like a stalled single-leg or double-leg attack. They duplicate what any wrestler could face in an actual match.

PHOTO 7-20: Fix position from one knee.

PHOTO 7-21: Tripod position ready to circle up.

PHOTO 7-22: Circle up into a good stance.

PHOTO 7-23: A stalled single on one knee.

PHOTO 7-24: Single-leg attack from the tripod position.

PHOTO 7-25: Circle up with the leg to the finish.

Activity

2. Position and Hand Fight

    –Face off (see Photo 7-26)

    –Back-to-back (see Photo 7-27)

    –Side to side (see Photo 7-28)

    –Kneeling vs. standing (see Photo 7-29)

    –Kneeling vs. kneeling (see Photo 7-30)

Purpose

A good stance is mandatory in the neutral position, and all wrestlers need work in maintaining a good position while simultaneously forcing an opponent/partner out of his stance.

This drill forces both wrestlers to focus on proper stance and motion while under constant pressure from an opponent.

At the whistle, wrestlers square off and battle for position. Both must sustain constant, forward, aggressive movement. (see Photos 7-31 & 7-32)

PHOTO 7-26

PHOTO 7-27

PHOTO 7-28

PHOTO 7-29

PHOTO 7-30

PHOTO 7-31

PHOTO 7-32

Activity

3. Level Change Drills

 —vs. the wall (see Photos 7-33 & 7-34)

 —vs. a partner (see Photos 7-35—7-38)

Purpose

A strong penetration step is crucial to any successful leg attack. Wrestlers should step only 8-12 inches (any farther could put them off-balance), bend their knees, and drive the hips forward. When they make contact with the wall of the partner, they must have their hips beneath them, and the trailing foot cannot pass the down knee.

PHOTO 7-33

PHOTO 7-34

PHOTO 7-35

PHOTO 7-36

PHOTO 7-37

PHOTO 7-38

Activity

4. Stance and Motion Drills

—vs. right foot lead

—vs. left foot lead

—Set ups and tie ups

Purpose

Wrestlers need to prepare for opponents who come at them in a variety of stances and directions. Wrestlers need to work at skills designed to force an opponent out of position and open for any leg attack. Head, hand, and foot fakes are important here. Coaches must remind wrestlers to move in all directions—forward, backward, laterally—and demonstrate this for them.

PHOTO 7-39: Inside control with both hands.

PHOTO 7-40: Collar tie and inside control.

PHOTO 7-41: Collar tie and wrist.

PHOTO 7-42: Underhook.

Activity

5. Boundary Drill

Purpose

When confronted by an opponent who plays the edge of the mat, a wrestler needs to know how to move him away from the boundary and open for a takedown attempt. He accomplishes this by angling his position to the boundary line and circling the opponent away from the edge.

DRILLS FOR THE NEUTRAL POSITION—DEFENSE

Activity

1. Sprawl Drills

    –from square stance

    –from staggered stance

2. Hip Down Drills (see Photos 7-43—7-45)

3. Snap and Spin (see Photos 7-46—7-49)

Purpose

Countering an opponent's quick-leg attack is vital in any wrestling match. Every wrestler should be prepared to turn a defensive maneuver into a scoring opportunity.

Here, the defensive man forces his hips down and back; his legs remain flexed and wide; his hands pressure the opponent's hand and arms.

Proper hip pressure forces the opponent's upper body down to the mat. The defensive man's hands and forearms block the opponent's shoulders and stop his penetration. An opponent stuck in this position becomes quickly exhausted and accessible to a defensive takedown (butt drag or snap & spin).

PHOTO 7-43: Stop the forward motion of the leg attack.

PHOTO 7-44: Drive hips down and widen the legs.

PHOTO 7-45: Force the chest on the opponent's head and his palms on the mat.

PHOTO 7-46: The offensive man takes an 80 percent shot, and the defensive wrestler blocks him.

PHOTO 7-47: The defensive wrestler gets hips down and feet back, putting pressure on the head.

PHOTO 7-48: He moves hip to hip.

PHOTO 7-49: He slides laces to laces and tightens up his control.

Activity

4. Hop and Balance (see Photos 7-50—7-55)

Purpose

When caught by a single-leg attack where his leg is elevated, a wrestler needs practice in recovering from this potentially damaging situation. Begin the drill with the offensive man already in control of a single leg. At the whistle he shoves the defensive man around his circle. The coach then shouts the command when the defensive man should initiate his countering movements as described below.

PHOTO 7-50: Caught by the single-leg attack, the defensive wrestler must maintain balance.

PHOTO 7-51: The offensive wrestler moves the defensive man around his circle, forcing him to hop on one foot.

PHOTO 7-52: The defensive wrestler grabs the elbows of his partner and works his hips beneath him.

PHOTO 7-53: The defensive wrestler moves his foot outside and shoves his hips down.

PHOTO 7-54: He forces his foot to the mat and pulls on the offensive man's elbows.

PHOTO 7-55: He circles away from the leg attack and positions himself in a good stance.

DRILLS FOR THE NEUTRAL POSITION—SEQUENCE DRILLING

Sequence drilling (wrestlers move from circle to circle on command from the coach) empowers wrestlers to think of attempting various takedown techniques in succession. They can make easier transitions from one maneuver to the next and become more conscious of planning several moves in advance. Through sequence drilling they are always moving and attempting various takedowns.

It is important that at each circle (station) they use motion, a set up, good penetration, and a strong finish. They should also alternate so that each wrestler has equal attempts.

Fireman's Carry

Single-leg attack and finish

Sprawl to front head-lock

Double-leg attack and finish

Sprawl to snap and spin

High crotch

DRILLS FOR THE TOP POSITION

Activity

1. "Froggy" (see Photos 7-56 & 7-57)

Purpose

A wrestler needs to learn how to use the force of his hips and upper body to drive an opponent off his base. In this drill, he should position himself like a frog—bent legs, bent arms, a hand on the opponent's hip and shoulder. He is permitted to use only the power of his hips and legs to shove his opponent (the arms are used only for balance).

PHOTO 7-56

PHOTO 7-57

Activity

2. "Float" Drill

Purpose

An opponent who frequently sits out or hip heists from the bottom can be difficult to control and pin. The offensive wrestler here follows the sit out—hip to hip, laces to laces—until the coach blows the whistle.

The offensive wrestler should never place his head over the opponent's shoulder, or drop his head too low to the mat.

Activity

3. Knee Pinch (see Photos 7-58 & 7-59)

Purpose

A quick drill which halts an opponent's stand up at the whistle. The offensive wrestler must use his knees to squeeze the ankles of the defensive wrestler. Keep in mind that the offensive man must then move quickly toward attempting a pinning hold.

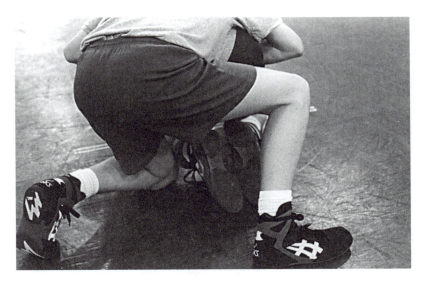

PHOTO 7-58

PHOTO 7-59

Activity

4. "Kick Him Out!" (see Photos 7-60—7-63)

Purpose

Wrestlers begin in the optional starting position. On the coach's whistle, the offensive wrestler pushes the upper hip of the defensive wrestler down and away and then circles away, preparing immediately to set up a takedown.

Wrestlers need to learn the proper procedure for releasing an opponent when in the top position and to gain confidence in achieving a takedown under any time limitations.

PHOTO 7-60: Proper optional starting position—note top man's bent arms and legs.

PHOTO 7-61: The offensive man shoves the defensive man to his hip.

PHOTO 7-62: The offensive wrestler moves towards the opponent's feet.

PHOTO 7-63: He then should move in quickly to set up a takedown.

Activity

5. Boundary Drill (see Photos 7-64—7-66)

Purpose

A potential fall could be lost if an opponent can push himself out of bounds. Here, wrestlers begin in any pinning combination near the boundary. The offensive wrestler must turn the defensive wrestler's head toward the center, his feet toward the boundary, and then tighten the pin hold.

PHOTO 7-64

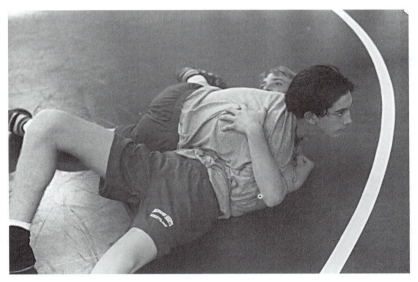

PHOTO 7-65

PHOTO 7-66

DRILLS FOR THE BOTTOM POSITION

Activity

1. Back-Back Drill (see Photos 7-67—7-70)

Purpose

Strong back pressure is crucial to completing a stand up and escaping from the bottom, yet too many kids are unaccustomed to moving backwards skillfully. This drill helps them master proper back pressure and hip position.

They should stick their backs against their partner's side and then use the power of their legs and hips to shove their opponent around their circle. It is important that their hips stay beneath them, that they do not put their hands on the mat, and that they do not become extended.

PHOTO 7-67: Initial starting position.

PHOTO 7-68: Shove the partner around the circle.

PHOTO 7-69: Never put palms on mat.

PHOTO 7-70: Never become extended.

Activity

2. Bridging Drill (see Photos 7-71—7-74)

Purpose

Getting pinned is a wrestler's worst insult. Even the champion can find himself suddenly caught on his back. If it does happen all wrestlers need to know how to get off their backs quickly and into a better position to escape.

PHOTO 7-71: Bridge to the crown of the head.

PHOTO 7-72: Slide an elbow hard underneath.

PHOTO 7-73: Hip heist to a tripod position.

PHOTO 7-74: Circle up from the tripod to a good stance.

Activity

3. Elevation Drill (see Photos 7-75—7-80)

Purpose

Completing a stand up escape depends on the wrestler going from the base position to his feet and staying there. However, when he gets to his feet, regardless of his quickness, an opponent can lift him off the mat.

Wrestlers, therefore, must remain alert to the possibilty of being lifted off the mat.This drill prepares wrestlers for this situation and teaches them how to readjust in order to complete the original stand up.

PHOTO 7-75: On the whistle the bottom man pops into a standup.

PHOTO 7-76: The offensive wrestler wraps around his middle and lifts him off the mat.

PHOTO 7-77: The bottom man keeps his knees together and lifts them to his chest.

PHOTO 7-78: The bottom man lands on his knees and brings his hips beneath him.

PHOTO 7-79: He immediately pops back to his feet and reaches for hand control.

PHOTO 7-80: He gets hand control and prepares to cut through the bodies.

Activity

4. Find the Hands Drill (Photos 7-81—7-83)

Purpose

Getting hand control of the offensive (top) wrestler is mandatory for any wrestler who wants to escape from the bottom. This drill empowers wrestlers to gain control of the top wrestler's hands without the need to look for them.

On the whistle, the offensive wrestler slides his hands to grab an ankle, tightens his grip on the defensive man's waist, or reaches for an underhook.

This drill teaches the bottom wrestler for this situation and prepares him how to locate the opponent's hands by sensing them on various areas of his upper body. He can learn how to readjust and complete his original escape.

PHOTO 7-81

PHOTO 7-82

PHOTO 7-83

Activity

5. Pop Ups (Photos 7-84–7-85)

Purpose

Explosiveness is crucial to escaping from the bottom, and wrestlers need a drill that increases their leg power and teaches them correct form. In this drill, wrestlers move from their base position to a stance position in one quick movement. Constant repetition is necessary here.

PHOTO 7-84

PHOTO 7-85

POWER COURSE

The "Power Course" offers (1) an intense form of conditioning for the wrestlers; (2) a different format for building strength and endurance; and (3) an effective method for evaluating everyone's stamina.

The "Power Course" consists of various stations (determine the exact number based on your number of participants) located in the wrestling room, gymnasium, weight room, and/or hallway. Wrestlers move without rest from station to station until each one has completed the circuit twice (or three times).

Typical stations are pullups, rope climbs, sprints, situps, step ups on bleachers, and pushups (see Photo 7-86). But you can create your own Power Course arranged according to the layout of your gymnasium.

PHOTO 7-86

Key Points

1. Alternate stations for specific muscle groups—i.e., do not have wrestlers using their arms, for example, at two straight stations. Have them move from an activity that builds arm strength to one that improves cardio-vascular endurance.

2. Allow 20-30 seconds at each station and a ten second transition period between stations. Conduct the Power Course for 15-30 minutes maximum.

3. Design the Power Course to fit your facilities, making sure that wrestlers do not interfere with teammates in their stations at any time.

4. Wrestlers must work with a partner.

5. Check with other coaches and the athletic director if you use any facility outside the wrestling room (weight room, stairways, hallways, etc.).

6. Be sure all wrestlers are supervised at all stations.

Typical Activities

1. Partner Squats
2. Sprints
3. Pushups
4. Partner Carries
5. Pull ups/Chin ups
6. Step ups on a bench
7. Rope Climbs
8. Pop ups
9. Partner lifts
10. Situps
11. Jump ropes
12. Dumbbell Curls
13. Spin drill
14. Position and Hand Fight
15. Competitive Takedowns
16. Hop Overs
17. Bear Crawls/Crab Walk
18. Leg lifts

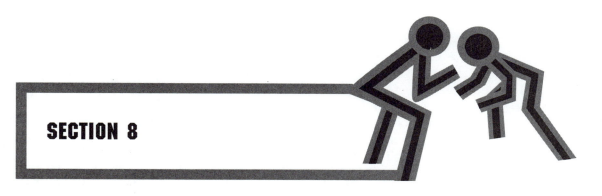

SECTION 8

Creating Championships

There is no harm in wanting to win. It is natural, even beneficial, to strive to win in competition. All coaches work to achieve championships for their teams and themselves. In fact, it is expected that they try to do so. Such expectations can give the team's efforts purpose and direction.

One varsity wrestler identifies his focus as an athlete: "I enjoy playing sports with my friends, but I participate for the awards of trophies and medals." A college wrestler adds: "Right now I'm only into it to qualify for Nationals." Phil DiRuggiero, from the Olmsted Falls Middle School wrestling team, is even more direct: "I want to take first."

The key word here is "creating." Coaches must create a championship much like an author composes an award-winning book or an artist paints on a canvas. The coach's best skills, insights, and efforts are required if winning a championship is the goal.

TEACH ATHLETIC ACHIEVEMENT

The wrestling coach is certainly a teacher, and his wrestlers are the students. It is up to the coach to provide a structured atmosphere for learning. He does this by using effective teaching methods, continuous evaluation, and positive feedback. He should always be ready to recognize his wrestlers' weak performances, diagnose their difficulties, and recommend improvements.

There are several ways to give feedback to wrestlers (ways that appeal to all learning styles) when evaluating their efforts towards producing a championship. One common way is to videotape the wrestler's performance and then view this later to analyze his strong and weak points. The coach can post stastistical charts (related to the wrestler's individual performance in recent competitions and over the season as a whole) that reveal clearly the wrestler's progress towards achievement (see Figure 4-1). A more time-consuming method is to offer each wrestler a written summary of his perfomance(s). The athlete can then add beneath the summary the steps he plans to take to improve his skills. A follow-up discussion can clarify what both coach and athlete can expect of each other. A final strategy for empowering wrestlers to win championships is a "hands-on" approach where the coach physically demonstrates the skills and works closely with the wrestlers to enable them to master the same skills. Whatever method you employ be sure your assessments of the wrestlers are accurate and lead to positive outcomes.

There is also much work to be done outside the practice room to produce a championship. The coach should display his team's accomplishments (a display case) for all to see, and arrange for the school newspaper to publish articles about members of the team. He can request statisticians complete a scrapbook for each senior wrestler who receives it at the awards program. When scheduling, the coach should arrange competitions, especially tournaments, where his kids can compete at their level. This enables them to be successful and to maintain confidence.

Designing achievement begins with the coach. You have to be hard working and set a solid example. You can be friendly with a wrestler, but he has to know that you will not let him take shortcuts. When an athlete discovers that you are dedicated toward his success, achievement is often likely to happen. This type of commitment on your part prompts wrestlers to be loyal to you and your program.

DISPLAY A WINNING PERSONALITY

The coach must also convey a winning personality, one that invites friendships and promises sincerity. When you demonstrate confidence in yourself and your wrestlers, you discover the power of charisma. You don't have to be movie-star charming, but you do have to be honest.

A winning coach sets high standards. This kind of coach succeeds because he expects to succeed. When a negative belief enters his mind (for example, "These kids just can't stop anyone from escaping") he quickly replaces it with a positive one ("Okay then, we're going to be the best team in the conference at takedowns"). This may appear to be a Pollyanna-ish approach, but this mind set is characteristic of all successful people. This type of outlook on a practical level requires you to

☑ analyze your situation—e.g., the team has difficulty riding opponents;

☑ design an advantage—e.g., we'll work harder on takedown skills; and

☑ believe enthusiastically that the plan will succeed—e.g., we'll total more takedowns than our opponents in every conference match.

Furthermore, these high standards must relate to a plan of action (your practice activities) that is clearly and concisely expressed to the entire coaching staff and then to the team. Completing these actions with enthusiasm and diligence becomes everyone's priority. Defining success and discussing strategy with the wrestlers each day (5 minutes) affirms their acceptance of those standards. Repetition of these affirmations leads to mastery. It also keeps wrestlers focused.

Most coaches already have the basic characteristics of a winning, competitive personality. They know how to present themselves as cheerful, considerate, and positive individuals. When a coach responds to his wrestlers in these ways, he gets better results from them on the mat.

Several athletes echo such sentiments. When asked what produces athletic achievement, here is what they said:

"The coach has to believe in me and give me a chance."

"The coach has to be patient. My coaches taught me self-control."

"My performance improved because my coach had faith in me."

"My coach kept pushing me to greater achievements and setting even higher goals."

"They were my role models, and they made me strive to be my best."

"Our strength and conditioning coach made the greatest difference for me. [He] made me run and lift weights when I didn't want to. At times I thought he was a jerk. Now, I have the utmost respect for this man."

I can honestly say I owe all my success to him."

"They don't let you quit when they know you can do it."

Team and individual achievement can be reinforced if you practice the principles and follow the guidelines outlined here. Creating the circumstances that make winning happen is certainly challenging and ongoing. Each season may require new methods, but the experienced coach realizes this. Each season means you have a new team (seniors have graduated, newcomers have joined), a fresh group to teach to win. Just be careful not to sabotage your success by being overconfident and overestimating your team's strengths or to base achievement on any one match or season.

DEAL WITH OVERACHIEVERS AND UNDERACHIEVERS

Evaluate the attitude toward winning seen in the following statements made by high school varsity wrestlers:

"I love to be the best at something, the feeling of dominating an opponent, of being a part of a championship team. After all, no one plays to lose."

"I compete because it gives me self-accomplishment. I'm always pushing myself to be the best."

"I think the experience of competing in sports and other activities will help me in the future. It's fun to do and keeps me active with others."

Do you recognize any underachievers here? Probably not. Each seems very self-motivated and eager to perform to his potential, yet each also has a very different reason for wanting to win. The first quote comes from a wrestler who needs victories or championships to justify his effort on the wrestling mat. The second athlete finds reward in simply improving himself. He seeks achievement only as a means to measure his personal improvement. Finally, the third speaker's gratification comes from a type of achievement that is almost social in nature—Winning is fun because it strengthens relationships.

Coaches have to be keen observers here. They need to identify each athlete's level of desire for success. Certainly, this relates back to the issue of commitment, but the wrestler's interest in competing also needs to be assessed. When a coach does this he can make some significant distinctions between the overachievers and underachievers on his team. The next key step is to enable those identified as underachievers to reach their full potential.

Test your wrestlers according to the following scale:

3 = VERY HIGH   2 = MODERATE   1 = VERY LOW

Use the following criteria (see Figure 8-1):

1. Enthusiasm—always hustling

2. Leadership—takes command in tough situations

3. Attentiveness—never needs directions repeated

4. Cheerfulness—easy to get along with

5. Punctuality—always on time for practice and meets

6. Dependability—never needs reminders to complete tasks

7. Conditioning—endurance during an entire match

8. Skill level—from neutral, bottom, and top

9. Ability to focus—never distracted during competition

10. Competitiveness—really enjoys competing

An athlete who scores in the 23–30 range is probably competing near the top of his potential regardless of his level of talent while those in the 16–22 range are achieving only 50–60 percent of their potential. In fact, you might choose to utilize this criteria and rating system with the wrestler to help him recognize that he is competing below his potential, but allow him to rate himself first. For example, when Greg Hellickson lost his first wrestle-offs at Olmsted Falls High School, his coach used the criteria to review his performance. "It didn't bother me," Greg says, "because there is always somebody better than me out there so there is always room for improvement. The coach told me to come back and try again the next week. He showed me how to be competitive, the wrong and right way to do things. I came back and won the next wrestle-off."

But what about those wrestlers who never seem to fulfill their potential? You may hear from them, "I can't win. He [the opponent] is too good." This type of wrestler is often an erratic performer who looks like a champion one day and a chump the next. For him, the underlying problem often is an intense fear of not measuring up, of not performing successfully in the next competition. It may be that they dread being successful although they are aware that their teammates and coaches are ready to congratulate them for any achievment.

Some wrestlers just want to be members of the team. Since they care little about success, they don't want to be responsible for winning. In this way, these underachievers can avoid blame or criticism. An important duty for a coach, then, is to prepare his wrestlers for triumph, especially those kids who only have infrequent experiences with success. He needs to define success for them.

RECOGNIZE ACHIEVEMENT IS IN THE EYE OF THE BEHOLDER

"One of the best experiences I have had has been to watch competition in the Special Olympics. It makes me feel good to see how happy every participant is at the finish of the race . . . . This is the proper perspective: Trying to do your best, learning about your limits, and then attempting to extend them."

—(FROM MIKE KRZYZEWSKI, DUKE UNIVERSITY BASKETBALL COACH)

Achievement can have nothing to do with wins. It can have no relationship at all to the numbers on the scoreboard. Coaches could, in fact, never base it on outcomes. Coaches need to see achievement defined in as many ways as they have wrestlers. They also should

☑ reward effort, not success;

☑ publicize ability, not outcomes;

☑ ensure the wrestlers see victory as theirs (or the team's), not the coach's;

☑ share losses with the wrestler; and

☑ respect the performance of all wrestlers.

If a coach can do this, he can identify achievement in all his wrestlers. Then he should build on that. Winning should never be a repeated goal; instead, select individual performance skills as goals because they relate more to the wrestler's self-motivation and personal achievement. "My accomplishment was just making it through the season," says one varsity wrestler who was winless during his sophomore season. A teammate adds: "I achieved success by setting personal goals for myself and knowing I reached them."

CREATE A WINNING ATTITUDE

Don't expect your wrestlers to walk onto the mat at the beginning of the season with a perfect positive attitude where they are eager to learn, excited about success, and ready to work hard. The coach has to nurture a winning attitude. Here are fifteen strategies:

1. Get to know athletes personally but do not violate their privacy.

2. Be sure each wrestler knows his value to the team.

3. Avoid false compliments.

4. Use their first names in practice.

5. Give them simple responsibilities.

6. Use terms like "Our team . . ." and "We're on track . . . ."

7. Maintain a positive attitude and make positive comments continually during practice and contests.

8. Highlight positive accomplishments (see Figure 8-2).

9. Discuss regularly the team's goals.

10. Offer constructive feedback on their performances.

11. Consider always their psychological and emotional needs.

12. Keep tension to a minimum, and practice relaxation techniques.

13. Be firm, but never harsh or domineering.

14. Keep kids focused on what they still can accomplish, not on what they failed to do before.

15. Teach kids how to enjoy competitions.

"He who believes is strong; he who doubts is weak.
Strong convictions precede great actions."

> **—(FROM J. F. CLARKE, AUTHOR)**

Mental toughness is essential to success. You've
got to be mentally tough. Mental toughness is many
things and rather difficult to explain. Its qualities
are sacrifice and self-denial. Also, most importantly,
it is combined with a perfectly disciplined will that
refuses to give in. It's a state of mind—you could
call it character in action."

> **—(FROM VINCE LOMBARDI)**

A winning, competitive attitude surfaces when the coach can give each wrestler a challenging yet realistic incentive to practice hard and compete aggressively. New challenges are then offered each time a task has been completed.

"My wrestling coach always wants us to push
ourselves to the edge. He treats it more as
the rule than the exception. He wants 110 percent."

> **—(FROM A VARSITY WRESTLER)**

REALIZE FAILURE IS A WORD; WINNING IS AN ATTITUDE

You might have wrestlers on your team who continually claim injuries—real or imagined, minor or major—in order to avoid competition. To these types of athletes, the match is more threatening than the hurt they may have. Some may try, like the WW II Japanese Kamikaze pilots, to become injured since only an injury can provide them some of the psychological nurturing they cannot receive elsewhere. In this way, the wrestler gets sympathy, relief from the competition, attention for the injury, and possibly a heroic stature in the eyes of his peers. This is the kid who exaggerates a limp or grimaces at the slightest touch. All of these actions often are intended to cover up a lack of confidence. In addition, the wrestler could be trying to punish himself for failing to reach a goal or live up to expectations. He is simply afraid to fail.

The coach needs to understand both this wrestler's fear of losing in the competition and his feelings of inferiority. Effective strategies would be to keep him at practice where he can train his healthy body parts, work at weak points, and build confidence ("You're showing some real strength there, just keep doing your best"). The wrestler has to realize that losing only adds weight to his life if he lets it. He can still be a "winner" no matter what the scoreboard indicates after the match.

Also, do not reprimand any wrestler for faking an injury. If this is the case, the athlete is sending an obvious signal that there is a more serious problem below the surface, often a personal one that may have nothing to do with you, the team, or the sport. Communication and understanding are the keys here to straightening out this type of problem and redirecting the athlete's attitude toward having a successful season.

Coaches need to be prepared to accept any wrestler's anxieties toward losing. According to one junior varsity wrestler, the coach has to "care and believe in everyone no matter how bad you are." A college wrestler describes his wrestling coach as "hard working. He puts kids first. He teaches what it takes to win, how to *mentally* win."

Always show genuine interest in your athletes' welfare; make it clear that you consider them important, that they are not just another spoke in the wheel on the team. Athletes develop at different levels and times through their careers, and sometimes teaching too much too fast can overwhelm a wrestler. The key here is to provide all wrestlers with meaningful and rewarding experiences, to help them see that losing a wrestling match only proves what didn't work that match. Winning is found in a person's character, not on a scoreboard.

PREPARE EFFECTIVELY FOR A MATCH OR TOURNAMENT

Getting athletes ready to compete requires their preparation physically, mentally, and emotionally. Here are their comments:

"I like competition. It makes me feel good. But I know I need my coach's help. I need him to fix my mistakes."

"I feel the coach has to be rough on his players, yet very personal. He may scream a lot, but he's gotta be understanding."

"The coach has to make me discipline myself both in and out of school."

"My coaches have always been guiding me in the right direction. They keep my goals high, and they get close to the kids on the team."

"My coach taught me that if you mentally win a match, your body will follow. He's enthusiastic and full of spirit. I learned that if you put your mind to something you can accomplish it."

"An effective coach must be a powerful speaker and be inspiring, along with great knowledge of the sport."

"The coach has to know what's best for me. He has to be a caring person and a loyal friend."

"A good coach knows how to train a team not just physically but also mentally to prepare to be the best. All my coaches have made me smarter and a better athlete through excellent training. They have worked my talents."

Key Point #1—Physical Preparation

Young athletes have to be told that getting in shape means experiencing various levels of discomfort. No one likes to work to exhaustion, yet wrestling does require daily doses of fatigue. You probably have discovered that working your wrestlers too hard in practice discourages some kids, but working them too lightly leaves them physically unprepared for competitions. Is there a happy medium?

Kids can find practice to be an enjoyable and enriching experience, regardless of its difficulty, if you . . .

- ☑ occasionally let team leaders run practice;
- ☑ list examples of matches where their physical conditioning has resulted in victory;
- ☑ point out how tapping into physical reservoirs of energy produces power;
- ☑ monitor their effort and its value to learning and improvement;
- ☑ have them pretend that "Today is our last practice of the season. Make it your best!"
- ☑ use a variety of drills; and
- ☑ know when to push and when to call it a day.

Take Carl Lewis, for example, probably one of the best track athletes of all time. When an interviewer asked Tom Tellez, his coach, to summarize the factors that prompted Lewis' phenomenal success, he said, "I attribute his success to his parents, his home life, and his stability. . . I don't like to overwork kids. I work on mechanics. You prepare the athlete mentally by preparing him physically."

Key Point #2—Mental Preparation

A veteran coach and Ohio Wrestling Hall of Fame member relates an interesting story about the power of mental preparation: Minutes before one of his less-talented wrestlers was to step onto the mat against a wrestler who had already placed in the state tournament, he lied and claimed that the opponent was terrible and deserved to be pinned. "The kid believed me without hesitation," he remembers, "and wrestled hard for six minutes trying to pin that other guy. After he won by a point, he apologized to me for not getting the pin. That's when I told him the truth and why I lied. Had he known the true caliber of his opponent he might have mentally prepared himself to lose, but when he believed the other guy was lousy he really felt he could win. Instead of getting killed out there by a more highly-skilled opponent, he earned three team points in a dual meet where every point counted."

A coach need not lie to prepare his wrestlers mentally for a competition, but he does have to use some psychological techniques. One way to begin is to have your wrestlers model themselves after the most successful competitor in your area, in your league, or on your own team. How does he mentally prepare himself? How does he behave? What does he do? Champion wrestlers stay poised and under control even during the most stressful situations on the mat. They don't fear the crowd, the challenge, or the opponent. Modeling is one way to learn, and following the example of a wrestler who always expects the best results and remains positive can be very effective.

Discussions about mental preparation should also take place during selected practices. It's possible that some kids may not be excited about an upcoming match or its outcome. The coach needs to explain the special purpose of an upcoming meet— How does it differ from the others? How do the coaches expect the team to perform? Why is achievement especially important here? Without accepting a purpose or objective for a competition, the wrestlers may feel like they're on a treadmill, working up a sweat but going nowhere.

An essential element to mental preparation is to remove the tension associated with taking a risk. The coach can create problem scenarios in practice—"You're losing by three points, you're in the neutral position, and there are only twenty seconds to go in the final period. What do you do?"—and invite his wrestlers to solve them, encouraging them to be unafraid to take the risk that could result in victory.

Here are six tips every coach should employ to complete his athletes' mental preparation:

1. Make your wrestlers familiar with what may be unfamiliar to them (i.e., play loud music in practice to simulate crowd noise).

2. Stress that they always stay under control and concentrate during a competition.

3. Remind them about what they can and cannot eat to remove anxieties about making weight.

4. Be sure they are knowledgeable about the weigh-in times, their opponent(s), and any other information associated with that competition (for example, if it is a double-elimination or single-elimination tournament).

5. Discuss their expectations and share the coaches' expectations.

6. Demand they listen to coaches, captains, and officials.

"The word 'If' should be eliminated from a wrestler's vocabulary. I hear so many athletes lamenting their lack of success by its use: 'If I had more strength; if I had better technique; if I had a better coach; If I had more experience.'

The success that U.S. wrestlers have achieved to date has been achieved because these individuals accepted responsibility, dedicated themselves to excellence and utilized whatever physical characteristics with which they were endowed."

—(FROM STAN DZIEDZIC, FORMER NATIONAL WRESTLING COACH)

Key Point #3—Emotional Preparation

Former Dallas Cowboy quarterback Roger Stauback declares, "Every time I stepped on the field, I believed my team was going to walk off the winner, somehow, some way." It is this kind of self-image, ambition, and focus we want our wrestlers to possess when they step onto the mat. However, most young people are victims of their own moods and emotions, which hinder their ability to deal effectively with the stress of competition.

Emotions in any extreme only impair an athlete's ability to eliminate distractions or to perform technical skills. The strongest emotion is fear, especially the fear of an uncertain outcome. Therefore, it is important for you to explain that every competition involves uncertainty. This shouldn't be feared. It should be enjoyed. Winning in wrestling is especially exciting when it occurs against an opponent who possesses equal or greater ability. Your wrestlers can improve their emotional preparation if you assist them in administering a self-evaluation beforehand. Help them take pride and pleasure in their personal achievements and clarify their strong points. The unfortunate reality is that most kids can list more of their weaknesses than their strengths, so the wise coach should comment on their winning qualities: "I like your hustle. That kind of effort will help you win this weekend" or "Your stand up is getting quicker. That's why you're leading the team in escapes over the last four matches" (Note that these statements are both affirmative and specific).

Before matches it is important to deal with their behavior (respectful and dignified) but avoid lecturing about their shortcomings. This only lessens your wrestlers' acceptance of their ability to succeed. Instead, emphasize their strengths and boost their self-esteem. Encourage teammates to support each other; viewing the team as a "family" helps everyone succeed.

If team members still appear troubled or upset, release this psychological burden by sharing it with them. Counter any negative feelings by giving them reasons to be excited about the upcoming competition and reviewing team (and possibly individual) goals.

"If I could have one hope for our young people as they go out into the world, it would be this: I hope they fail. I hope they fail at something that is important to them, for failure, like nothing else, is able to stimulate the right kind of person to that extra action that always makes all the difference."

—(FROM LYMAN FERTIG)

Key Point #4—The Close Matches

These are the one- or two-point matches that make even the best of us tense. It is up to the coach, however, to prepare wrestlers for these kinds of matches, and if he does an effective job they should triumph most of the time.

Here are my instructions to my wrestlers:

1. Keep your mouth shut and look over at every break (referee's whistle).

2. Stay focused on basic techniques and prompt your opponent into making a mistake.

3. Force your opponent into a position where he is basically unfamiliar (refer back to the scouting report).

4. In the neutral position, if you can't get your opponent opened up for a take-down, get him called for stalling.

5. Never waste energy chasing, lunging, or worrying—just be persistent.

In any match I coach, my comments are always brief and calm. I use my hands as much as possible instead of my voice since no crowd can ever drown out the message I deliver that way. For example, both thumbs up means "You're doing fine, keep trying the same technique." Lifing and dropping my hands palm down toward the mat means "Ride him and look for the pin." A tap on my leg and then my neck tells my wrestler to ride with the legs and use the power half.

If I do shout it often is only to remind them of the score, the remaining time, or their proximity to the boundary. I want them focused on the opponent, not any yelling from me or the fans. I think this shift away from a dependency on me to guide them through each step of a match gives them confidence through any close match.

Key Point #5—Handling Setbacks

"The superior man blames himself. The inferior man blames others."

—(FROM DON SHULA, MIAMI DOLPHINS COACH)

Sometimes failure has little to do with our physical talents. It just happens. Kids have to understand that failure can only harm them if they let it, if they let it affect their psyche.

Everyone makes mistakes, but the better competitors don't make excuses. The very best wrestlers take responsibility for their losses, correct their mistakes, and move on. They don't blame others, nor do they dwell on the loss. More importantly, these athletes return to the wrestling room with an immediate incentive to improve their weak points. "It may sound strange," says Bob Richards, an Olympic gold medalist in the pole vault, "but many champions are made champions by setbacks. They are champions because they've been hurt. Their experience moved them, and pulled out this fighting spirit, making them what they are."

"A man who has committed a mistake and doesn't correct it is committing another mistake."

—(FROM CONFUCIUS)

"The child's philosophy is a true one. He does not despise the bubble because it burst; he immediately sets to work to blow another one."

—(FROM J.J. PROCTOR, AUTHOR)

Key Point #6—Handling Success

For some people, achievement is accompanied by anxiety. A winning coach faces the pressure of staying successful, of repeating a championship, of setting new standards of excellence. Though victory can be exhilarating, success can present a fresh set of problems.

The most prominent difficulty is re-creating the achievement. After you have won the "big" match or even the state tournament, fans and/or administrators may expect these accomplishments every wrestling season. Some coaches then find themselves struggling not to lose rather than striving to win.

Another problem could be reacting to excessive praise. You revel in these compliments and ignore constructive criticism. That type of response is a mistake. The late Howard Ferguson, whose St. Edwards High School teams won seven national high school championships, offers the best advice: "Self-praise is for losers. Be a winner. Stand for something. Always have class and be humble. When you win, say nothing; when you lose, say less."

"If you achieve success, you will get applause, and if you get applause, you will hear it. My advice to you concerning applause is this: enjoy it, but never quite believe it."

—(FROM ROBERT MONTGOMERY, POET)

Finally, success means goals were accomplished, but it does not mean that all mistakes have been eliminated. No match is wrestled perfectly. A discerning, analytical coach first reviews the elements that resulted in victory and then anticipates his next opportunity to repeat them. He is not satisfied with one winning season or one tournament title. He remains eager to empower his wrestlers again with the strategies and skills that made success occur the first time. Legendary football coach Don Shula cautions us that "success isn't final. Past performance is forgotten in every new competition. It is harder to stay on top than it is to get there."

Key Point #7—Pre-Meet Conduct

Important points here revolve around effective communication. Your wrestlers need a consistent, structured approach that leaves them relaxed and prepared.

Be sure to address the following ten items:

1. how you expect them to behave on the bus, in the locker room, and on the mat;

2. why they should never talk during the weigh-in, to their opponent, or toward the crowd;

3. how to check their alignment with the official;

4. when they should exit the locker room and line up for introductions;

5. how team members should support each other during the meet;

6. what to eat before and after the meet;

7. why the captains rule the locker room if a coach is not present;

8. how to get focused prior to their matches;

9. when they should warm-up;

10. why it is important the last person they talk to before wrestling and the first person they talk to after wrestling is the coach.

You can distribute a handout to your wrestlers the week before the first match that clarifies each of these items (see Figure 8-4).

Key Point #8—Dealing with Referees

Regarding officials, coaches from all ranks often find it easy to blame them for a disappointing outcome after a competition. Some coaches enjoy chastising an incompetent official while the official, in turn, satisfies himself by accusing the coach of unsportsmanlike behavior and threatening to penalize him. At no time has it ever been written that coaches and officials are adversaries. Ironically, both have the same goal: a safe, well-wrestled match with the winner to be determined fairly on the mat.

Never let your kids witness you blaming an official for a loss because that sets a precedent they will follow. Instruct your wrestlers that although incompetent officials may exist, they should never determine the outcome of their matches. Complaining about bad calls only ruins your concentration and disrupts your wrestler's performance. Even brooding about it afterwards gets you nowhere.

Through the season(s), familiarize yourself with the referees in your area and their style of officiating. Let them get to know you and your style of coaching. After the official has checked your team in the locker room, ask him how he might call a certain situation—stalling, for example. If you need to speak to the official during the match, do it the correct way and approach the scorer's table. Make requests, not arguments. Ask about the score, not his judgment.

There always needs to be an understanding between the two groups, and that begins with effective communication. But keep in mind that bingo is the only competition you win with talking.

DEFINE DISCIPLINE AND CREATING CONSEQUENCES

Practice involves wrestlers functioning together as a group or, at least, in pairs. Since a group effort is required, group rules are needed. The individual wrestler, therefore, becomes responsible to the group, and a key to teaching that responsibility is to teach discipline.

Discipline does not have to be intimidation or anger. It does not necessarily refer to a set of rules and regulations. Discipline simply suggests the standards by which the group is going to operate. Consider for a moment the coach who trains five athletes and the coach who trains fifty. Both will have different responsibilities for their athletes and different needs.

Consider: Is discipline just a means to maintain order? To restrict unwanted behavior? Is it punishment?

Researchers indicate that when discipline is perceived as punishment, it only serves to pressure athletes. Effective discipline, on the other hand, gets wrestlers ready to handle the stress of competition. Effective discipline is seen as a positive, almost beneficial influence in the wrestler's life. Stephan Terebienic competed in varsity football and wrestling at St. Edwards High School where he earned an individual state title. He credits his success to coaches who were "tough, strict, and demanding." Disciplined wrestlers are easy to coach because they follow team and school rules and make themselves amenable to instruction.

Call this psychological conditioning. Every time any kind of group comes together, rules and guidelines need to be established. You would be wise to:

☑ begin psychological conditioning on the first day;

☑ explain what behavior is acceptable and what isn't;

☑ reward behavior that leads to successful performances;

☑ get the athletes to believe that the rules are important; and

☑ modify inappropriate behavior individually but stress continually that you are operating under the premise of what is best for the team and the program.

What kind of rules do you need? There are certainly those sport specific rules (like the illegal slam) that you must follow, but you need additional guidelines for wrestlers to follow that govern their behavior and conduct as members of your team. These may include:

☑ attending all team meetings, practices, and competitions;

☑ abstaining from all nonprescription drugs, alcohol, and tobacco (all types);

☑ respecting all coaches, teammates, officials, opponents, and other school personnel;

☑ arriving on time for meetings, practices, and competitions (especially when transportation to another site is involved);

☑ acting well-behaved and polite and representing the school in a dignified manner;

☑ getting a coach's permission before exiting practice or leaving the site of a competition;

☑ maintaining eligibility (academics);

☑following all directions given by the coaching staff during any practice or competition;

☑replacing any lost or damaged equipment; and

☑reporting any injury immediately to a coach.

When the wrestlers respond in disciplined fashion, they should be rewarded. When they don't, their actions need to be addressed: How have those actions hurt the team, the athlete, or the coach? The wrestler deserves an explanation, and a goal-oriented team deserves to have that distraction removed. "The coach should always have the control and attention of his team," says Gavin Peterson, who has played on three varsity teams for University High School. "A coach should always stress discipline. He should not only make his players better players but better people at the same time."

When wrestlers violate team rules, the coaching staff must be prepared to administer consequences. Never use a physical activity as a form of punishment. If you use, for instance, sprints at the end of practice it is possible the wrestler will then equate sprints, which are an effective form of conditioning, with punishment and never run them with intensity. The same holds true with any other physical activity (I know a coach who made his wrestlers compete in 8-12 extra matches after practice if they got caught chewing gum in school, which made them stop chewing gum and start hating matches).

Instead, design your consequences to not only benefit the wrestler but also the entire team. Here are some activities they could do if they've violated a team policy:

1. mop and clean the wrestling mat;

2. pick up any trash in the wrestling room, gym, and locker room;

3. clean the training room floor, tables, and equipment;

4. scrub and disinfect headgears or other equipment;

5. clean a classroom or locker room.

If a wrestler still does not change his behavior or actions you would be wise to have a conference with the wrestler and his parents. Violations cannot be allowed to continue. These kinds of disruptions hinder everyone's opportunity to achieve success.

Effective discipline leads to effective practices. The coach, too, must be a disciplined person. He is the role model the wrestlers need to follow. The approach the coach takes should "parallel the philosophy of the school in general," advises Tom Bryan, director of athletics at Hawken School. "There has to be fair play and emotional stability on everyone's part. In the gym, in the pool or on the field, athletes soon learn whether they are able to control their emotions enough to be effective or whether their emotions are going to control them."

"I believe in discipline. You can forgive incompetence. You can forgive lack of ability. But one thing you cannot ever forgive is lack of discipline."

—(FROM FORREST GREG, FORMER NFL COACH)

*"Don't be afraid to remind any players who are
out of line or not in the spirit of your training
rules that they owe it to the school to straighten
themselves out. You win when everyone works
together as a team—never let one or two
players pull your whole team down."*

—(FROM PAUL BROWN, FORMER NFL COACH AND GENERAL MANAGER)

Be Ethical—You Be the Judge

The principles you establish for yourself determine your ethics. How important is following the rules of the sport? Which rules should be followed? Which ones can be ignored if ignoring them can benefit my team or my program?

It becomes a matter of integrity. If we are sincere about teaching our wrestlers to obey rules and wrestle fairly then we must do the same. This topic is so significant that three major Ohio colleges have semester courses in ethics alone. People, it seems, need training in how to be honest and ethical.

Some coaches may find it useful to address these principles regularly throughout the season, even weekly. One varsity wrestler respects his coach for speaking out about this. "He has also taught me how to overcome hardships," he adds, "how to take pride in the team, not to cheat ever. He's a strict coach."

If you want to be recognized for operating an honest program, you need to have strong ethics and character. The head coach needs to instruct assistants why integrity is important. The public must see the wrestling staff as individuals who take responsibility for their actions and refuse to compromise their values, even when the issue is unpopular or winning is put in jeopardy.

Even if you are desperate to win, you cannot violate ethical behavior. Cheating cheapens the value of winning; true glory comes when victory is achieved honestly and diligently.

There is a growing problem in many parts of the country where private or parochial schools recruit athletes away from the public schools. Many public school coaches cite this practice as unethical and unfair. According to Michael Verich, an Ohio legislator, "If this is going to become a bidding war over athletics or if it is going to become choosing one school over another because it has a better sports program, then we have lost sight of our objectives."

A coach has to develop in his athletes a sense of pride in a program that functions by the rules. They have to appreciate their own integrity and honor it in their opponents. This doesn't happen easily or quickly for most teenagers who rarely find fault with ignoring authority's rules. It is strongly recommended you spend the time to explain the importance of integrity to them. It may be a conversation you repeat often.

Honest actions must be a part of your program consistently. "Truth has no special time of its own," says Albert Schweitzer, the French physician. "Its hour is now—always."

FIGURE 8-1 ACHIEVEMENT ANALYSIS

Test your wrestlers' achievement according to the following scale:

3 = VERY HIGH   2 = MODERATE   1 = VERY LOW

Criteria   *Score*

1. Enthusiasm—always hustling   _____

2. Leadership—takes command in tough situations   _____

3. Attentiveness—never needs directions repeated   _____

4. Cheerfulness—easy to get along with   _____

5. Punctuality—always on time for practice and meets   _____

6. Dependability—never needs reminders to complete   _____
   tasks

7. Conditioning—endurance during an entire match   _____

8. Skill level—from neutral, bottom, and top   _____

9. Ability to focus—never distracted during   _____
   competition

10. Competitiveness—really enjoys competing   _____

Total Score   _____

FIGURE 8-2 HIGHLIGHTING ACCOMPLISHMENTS

Recognizing Team/Individual Achievements

Date _____

After any team or individual accomplishment follow the checklist below:

1. _____ Make a public address announcement in school

2. _____ Post a picture(s)—Wrestler of the Week—V/JV

3. _____ Give information to school newsletter director

4. _____ Have wrestler's locker decorated

5. _____ Post updated statistics on bulletin board

6. _____ View videotape in practice

7. _____ Contact media—newspaper, radio, television

8. _____ Inform administration and faculty

9. _____ Write personal congratulatory note

10. _____ Create highlight poster(s) for hallways

FIGURE 8-3 PRE-MEET GUIDELINES

Pre-Meet Guidelines

Below are the coaches' expectations of you before any competition:

A. The Day Before

1. Follow all diet instructions—no exceptions.

2. Get 8-9 hours of sleep.

3. Take a warm bath if you have trouble falling asleep.

4. Avoid eating any candy or pop since these foods can have strong effects on your metabolism and prevent you from falling asleep.

5. Relieve any tension by distracting yourself with watching television, attending another school function, or reading a book or magazine.

B. The Day of the Competition

1. Attend the assigned weight check.

2. Report on time for the competition.

   • FOR ANY HOME DUAL MEET always report one-and-a-half hours before the schedule match time (i.e., report at 5:30 P.M. for a 7:00 P.M. match).

   • FOR ANY AWAY DUAL MEET Always report fifteen minutes before the bus leaves (i.e., report at 4:45 if the bus departs at 5:00 P.M).

3. Assist with mat set up and break down for any home match.

4. Attend the competition and sit on or near the team bench if you are not competing.

5. Do not wear any unassigned t-shirt or striped socks.

6. Do not eat or drink anything without permission from a coach.

7. Never criticize the official at any point.

8. Follow all directions as instructed by any coach.

9. Do not leave the bench area unless permitted by a coach.

10. Never embarrass the team, your program, or yourself.

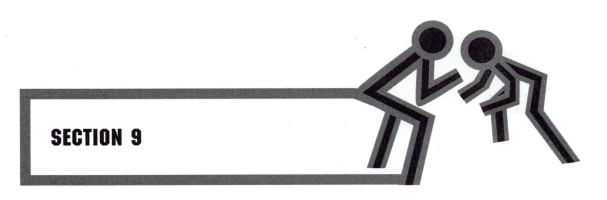

SECTION 9

Publicizing Your Program

Today's coaches have to realize that their work isn't completed after the practice or match has ended. An added duty that too many coaches leave unattended is publicizing their program. Effective public relations can have a significant influence on team success. The wrestlers' parents, the local media, school administrators, and fellow teachers all deserve to be informed about the team's progress through the season (and all year in some cases).

Coaches should satisfy the needs of these groups. Whether their involvement is direct or indirect, they can have a strong influence on team achievement. If you can establish a positive connection between these persons and the wrestling program, your position in the school and community becomes more prominent and the wrestling team itself becomes more popular. As before, effective communication is the key.

Publicity can appear in various forms and formats. At times, you might in a newsletter only convey basic information, like statistics, upcoming matches, or your "Wrestler of the Week" award winner; in other instances, like a speech, you could provide more personal items about team members, which could include any academic honors or their accomplishments in other sports. A colleague uses his "Miluk's Minutes," a newsletter that lists the significant details related to his program—tournament results, team picnic, fund raisers, rules clarifications—along with an interesting trivia question and a famous quote to keep his parents and fans informed and interested in his program.

Public relations and advertising are closely connected here. You are a salesman, and your product is your wrestling program. Your objective is to attract the attention of the people in your school and community and get them interested in your product. This has become a principal part of the coaching profession. Laura Keller, an assistant principal at Oak Harbor High School in Ohio, looks to hire a coach who has "the right attitude to work with the community, relate well to students and parents, and have some experience in public relations."

PUBLICIZING YOUR PROGRAM IN YOUR SCHOOL

Successful public relations for any wrestling program begins in the school itself. Gaining the support of the faculty for the team should be given the highest priority. To turn teachers into advocates of your program there are several things you can do:

1. Talk to them about the wrestlers and keep them informed about the team's progress. If they are anti-athletic, address it. Gain support by monitoring your wrestlers' academic standing in their classes and assisting them with their assignments.

2. Invite the teachers to attend competitions. Offer them free passes, if necessary, and thank them afterwards for attending.

3. Convince them of their importance to your program. Here, you can initiate an "Adopt-a-Wrestler" program where a faculty member can become the personal "cheerleader" for a wrestler on the team (write him notes, wish him luck, inquire about his matches, etc.).

4. Seek their advice when you confront a problem with a wrestler who has previously expressed a respect for that teacher. You might even request that this faculty member join a conference you might have with that wrestler.

5. Give each faculty member a free wrestling media guide (see Figure 9-1) or wrestling program. Send each one a copy of your newsletter.

6. Discuss the ancient origins of wrestling with the history teacher and the sport's appearance in literature with the English teacher (see Figure 9-2).

7. Invite the physical education teacher to put the team through an aerobic workout at the beginning of a practice early in the week.

8. Have the home economics teacher or school dietician design a menu for wrestlers who plan to lose weight.

9. Invite appropriate faculty members (possibly other coaches) to speak to the team about goal-setting, positive attitude, or successful people.

10. Have teachers complete an academic progress report each week for wrestlers who might have grade or eligibility problems in their classes (see Figure 9-3).

11. Ask the advisor to the school newspaper to have student reporters write articles about selected wrestlers.

12. Give each teacher a copy of your schedule and goals at the beginning of the season and ask that they spend a moment between classes to encourage any wrestler to achieve success in his matches and in accomplishing his goals.

13. Give each teacher a copy of your award winners at the end of the season so that they can congratulate them.

Your school administrators also need to be informed about the goals of the program and updated about the progress of the team. They also need to know that you are concerned about each athlete's academic standing. "A coach has to model a strong work ethic," says Harmon Middle School principal Jerry Brodsky, "and he has to promote scholarship in the classroom. I think it's also important that they have pride in the community."

The same principle is an essential focus for most parents as well. Karol Stewart, whose son competes on the varsity golf and wrestling teams, says, "I think the coaches should help him build his skills, but they better keep his training, winning, and studies in a proper perspective. I think the coaches should reaffirm what his father and I have been trying to tell him all along about his academics."

Administrators often need to be convinced that the coach is willing to be a "team player" himself within the school. Acknowledging school standards, adhering to its regulations, following the steps in the chain of command—all are important elements in forming a successful relationship with a school administration (principal, superintendent). Once the coach shows his support for the administration's policies, they in turn become quite enthusiastic about supporting the coach's program.

Mike Grose, athletic director at Norwalk High School, demands a "commitment to Norwalk High School" first from his coaches. "They have to follow the guidelines in the athletic handbook and they need to have strong communication skills, especially with parents, players, and the media. Also, much of how other schools feel about us is created by our teams and coaches."

"When I consider the effectiveness of a coach, I ask myself, 'Would I want this person coaching my kid?'"

—(FROM DR. HANS PESCH, PRINCIPAL)

Other groups and organizations within the school that can support and enhance your program are Spirit Groups or Pep Clubs; Cheerleaders; Statisticians; and the Student Council.

What can they do?

☑ make posters and displays in school hallways;

☑ organize pep assemblies and lead cheers;

☑ advertise your program in the school;

☑ increase the attendance at your games and tournaments;

☑ write up articles about your players for the school newspaper (or other publications);

☑ make announcements about the team and top performers;

☑ photograph your players and highlight them in school display cases;

☑ put a team schedule and pictures in community businesses and stores;

☑ pass resolutions (student government) praising the team and/or individual performers; and

☑ spread the word about your program.

It is important to get the student body on your side because with their support the team can become even more inspired to be successful. An effective way to boost the student body's interest and educate them about wrestling is to have an all-school assembly where you introduce all squad members and display wrestlers in action. You can use a videotape on a large screen, a slide show, or two boys who demonstrate an actual match that you choreograph beforehand.

Get the cheerleaders and Pep Club involved. Your guidance here should be minimal if each group's advisor is willing to participate in supporting your team. Attend one of their practices or meetings and explain how wrestling differs from the more traditional team sports. Then let them create their own cheers, signs, and banners. They might also provide beverages, snacks, or other treats after a match for the wrestlers. Later, be sure to publicly acknowledge and thank them for their efforts.

PUBLICIZING YOUR PROGRAM IN YOUR COMMUNITY

It is often heard from coaches who win a championship in any sport that winning that title was a "community effort." If people in the community can be persuaded to care about a team, they become eager to contribute to it. The coach's task, then, is to convince parents and citizens in the community to support his wrestling program.

Indeed, it is mandatory that the coach form a positive relationship with the wrestlers' parents. He can gain parental support by being available to discuss any wrestler's progress, providing technical information (usually about weight loss) in simpler terms, and regularly informing them (by newsletter) about any policies, events, or updates related to the team.

Here are a few things people can do to help:

☑ make small donations so you can purchase warm-ups, t-shirts, sports drinks, books, and videotapes for the team. Be sure to thank them afterwards (see Figure 9-4);

☑ provide transportation to summer camps and tournaments;

☑ bring friends and relatives to competitions to make a loud, strong, and united cheering section;

☑ work at a scoretable or ticket booth for home dual meets;

☑ provide after-match parties in their homes for the boys;

☑ assist the coaching staff by monitoring the boys' training habits and diets;

☑ encourage other boys to participate in the program at any level, which makes the team more competitive;

☑ add enthusiasm to the program, which in turn increases the popularity of wrestling in the school system.

What can you do to achieve community support? This list gives you a dozen ways to begin and may help you think of additional ideas.

1. Initiate a networking system where parents who are already involved with the program spread the word about it to their neighbors and friends.

2. Be sure the school newsletter highlights team accomplishments and profiles individual wrestlers.

3. Speak about your program to local organizations, like the Kiwanis and Rotary (and join these associations).

4. Attend the social functions arranged by the Booster Club or PTA.

5. Make yourself visible in the community—shop in local stores, eat in local restaurants, swim in the community pool.

6. Post the wrestling schedule in neighborhood stores and businesses and give a ticket to each owner or manager.

7. Have assistant coaches and varsity wrestlers spread the word about the program in the community.

8. Distribute a media guide through the school mailing system (see Figure 9-1).

9. Seek the support of the mayor and city council members by appearing at their meetings and talking to them individually.

10. Publicize the team and individual accomplishments through brochures or pamphlets published by city hall.

11. Invite the media to interview you and/or your better wrestlers.

12. Appear at school board meetings to announce updates about the team and individuals.

Gaining support from an entire community is certainly challenging and often slowly accomplished; however, do not be suprised by a snowball effect after you begin your efforts. Your own passion for your program can serve to inspire others to support it. Fostering enthusiasm for your wrestling team in both the school and general community may appear as an overwhelming challenge, but this responsibility cannot be neglected. "A coach for me has to have the ability to get along with parents and be cooperative," says James G. Bukes, athletic director at University High School. "There can't be any philosophical differences because athletics is a high visibility program and can be used as a very positive tool for the school."

Potential support groups in the community are the Kiwanis, Rotary, American Legion, Lions, Chamber of Commerce, and local churches. By obtaining the support of these clubs, a program may enjoy the financial and political support that most successful programs must have to prosper. Begin by writing a letter to the organization's president where you introduce yourself and the wrestling program—a brief history and current expectations. Explain in your letter how you may want them to contribute to the team—attending matches, making a donation, help host a special event (an all-star wrestling match, for example), or purchase some supplies. You should also request the opportunity to speak at their next meeting. A brief, enthusiastic speech can not only acquaint them with the sport of wrestling, it can also intensify their interest in your program.

Clearly, the most important community group is the Booster Club. Their funding, attendance at contests, and overall support are invaluable. You just need to be cautious of an over-zealous Booster Club, especially if the team is losing. Herbert Swender, an author who has written extensively about sports, acknowledges that the community plays a "major role in the development and growth of young people in interscholastic activities." Swender warns, however, that any kind of "negative talk should not be tolerated from the booster club . . . or citizens at large."

Booster clubs can perform many functions to assist coaches and/or the school's athletic department, but it is often unwise to involve them in activities related to a strategy for a competition or the training methods of the wrestlers. Great caution and scrutiny should also be given when excessive contributions are made, especially when money is involved. John Ralph, former basketball coach at Admiral King High School in Ohio, managed a 17-6 record in his first year and won Lorain County Coach of the Year honors in 1993. His booster club, however, was disappointed that the team's talent was wasted when it didn't advance farther in the state playoffs. Ralph was then accused of stealing club funds.

Ralph resigned, claiming he was tired of the hassle of dealing with booster club members who were dissatisfied with his coaching. He left, he said, with "mixed emotions." His case is still pending in court.

Be ready for other potential problems: A veteran (18 years) coach at an Illinois junior high school says, "Most of my disappointments have been with the parents who don't care or don't want their children involved. Or they want to control things too much." Jack Lesyk, Ph.D., a sport psychologist, warns that although parents may encourage their son to participate in wrestling, "they sometimes don't know how to do this effectively. Sometimes adults project their own unfulfilled dreams, motivations, and goals onto their children."

Such difficulties can be eliminated often through open and candid dialogues with parents. Lesyk recommends that the coach explain to parents how to talk to their son about his feelings about competition and achievement and how "to define success in terms of their attainment of their own goals." The parent should also "downplay winning and external rewards."

Lessen parents' questions and concerns by providing written information (see Figure 9-5) where these matters are answered. One avenue for distributing this information is a "Meet the Team" Night.

PRESENTING A "MEET THE TEAM" NIGHT

Host a "Meet the Team" Night at the beginning of the season the week before your first match. Invite to this gathering wrestlers, managers, statisticians, coaches, administrators, fans, faculty, the media, students, and parents.

Most parents are pleased when their son decides to join an interscholastic sport, and they are even more pleased when they can see and hear their son acknowledged in front of his peers. The "Meet the Team" event, best held on a weekday evening, accomplishes this.

A typical agenda for this event should take no more than one to one-and-a-half hours. You, as the head coach, should do the following:

1. Welcome those who attend and thank them for their recognition of the importance of the "Meet the Team" Night event.

2. Introduce the managers and acknowledge them for their daily contributions to the program.

3. Have the advisor to the statisticians introduce these individuals and clarify their duties during a dual meet or tournament.

4. Introduce your coaching staff and give the important backgrounds of each coach. Allow each coach to say a few words, if he is comfortable with speaking to a large group.

5. Explain the coaching staff's philosophy, goals, and expectations for each squad—the freshmen, junior varsity, and varsity. You should also explain your expectations of parents, which usually centers on the kind of behavior they should display in the stands (sportsmanship, enthusiasm, etc.).

6. Comment briefly on typical practice activities and the organization of wrestle-offs.

7. Display a slide show or videotape of the wrestlers in action in practice or at a scrimmage.

8. Allow a guest speaker(s) to make a presentation to the parents and wrestlers. Some possibilities here would be a sports psychologist, physical therapist, college coach or wrestler, a licensed nutritionist, and an experienced mother of a wrestler.

9. Invite the athletic director or principal to speak to the group.

10. Distribute an information packet that includes the practice and competition schedule, nutrition guide, and training rules.

11. Introduce, in order, the freshmen, junior varsity, and varsity teams, or organize the introduction by classes, beginning with freshmen and ending with seniors. Possibly allow the team captains to make a brief comment on their expectations for the season.

12. Conclude by thanking the fans and parents and offering your hope that the season will be a pleasant and memorable experience for them. Invite everyone to stay for any informal discussions and refreshments (select some mothers to arrange this for you).

Pat Elkins, who coaches little league in Danville, Virginia, holds such a meeting every year for the parents of her players. "You can't expect me to teach your kids good sportsmanship," she tells them, "if you're in the stands displaying poor sportsmanship. I won't hesitate to come up into the stands and ask you to leave." Elkins reports that in 16 years of coaching she has yet to have any problems. "I take a different view of coaching . . . I remember what it's like to cry and perhaps to have a difficult experience with sports at a young age. You can't just think of kids as little adults."

Later, hold a "Parents' Night" Match during the middle or at the end of the season. Here, prior to the dual meet, each boy escorts his parents into the gym as the announcer introduces them. An added highlight would be for each boy to present his mother with a single flower and his father with a t-shirt that match the school's colors.

DESIGNING AND DISTRIBUTING A NEWSLETTER

These types of correspondences are invaluable. They are the most effective way for any sports organization or school group to advertise its achievements and communicate to its athletes and fans. Newsletters are also a powerful tool for low-cost public relations that promote your program and create enthusiasm. They can be used to:

☑ build a sense of family within the team;

☑ improve wrestlers' performances by identifying their individual statistics;

☑ update the parents, fans, administration, and community on individual and team results;

☑increase your wrestlers and parents' loyalty and morale;

☑update administrators and parents on new rules, procedures, and/or techniques associated with wrestling;

☑convey any special promotional or motivational messages;

☑reduce potential complaints from parents or school personnel;

☑build your credibility and professional standing;

☑maintain the fans' interest in your program; and

☑create a positive image about you and your wrestlers.

No matter what type of newsletter you eventually design, you are conveying an important image to your wrestlers and the community (parents especially). Formats and styles of newsletters can vary (see Figure 9-6), yet each should provide some common information including the following items:

1. An introduction that grabs the readers' attention on the first page and keeps them reading

   Example

   Have our hearts recovered? Those nail-biting victories over Aurora and Newbury certainly caused the adrenalin to flow and the cheers to erupt. My kids—your kids—our kids were psyched and relentless. They demanded the victory and they got it! To be sure, your presence and support really helped make it happen.

2. Dual meet and tournament results

3. Upcoming matches

4. Updates or announcements about important events or honors that involve the team or individual wrestlers

   Example

   The team finished as United Press International's number one rated school in Division III for the season, which was determined by the votes of coaches across the state.
   The News Herald also ranked us number one in the area.

   Example

   Tickets for the state wrestling tournament are $21.00/packet and can be purchased from Coach Manos.

5. Individual statistics

6. Comments from assistant coaches and/or administrators

   Example

   "I'm enjoying the opportunity to coach these young student-athletes, yet I caution them to be 'doers' and not 'talkers.' We cannot relax but continue to strive toward becoming the best we can be." (from an assistant coach)

7. A wrestling trivia question

Example

What wrestler holds the record for most career wins at our school?

8. Inspirational quotes

Example

"Courage is not how a man stands or falls, but how he gets back up again." (from John L. Lewis)

9. Reminders (related to dates and times of special events or the collection of equipment and uniforms)

10. Public thank you's to administrators and/or parents

Example

Thanks to Mrs. Patricia Raiff, our principal, and Dr. Marc Crail, superintendent, for the dedicated support of our program. They remained constantly attentive to the needs of the coaching staff and showed a special understanding of our wrestlers. We owe our success in part to you.

Create (possibly use one of your more artistic athletes to assist you) a unique and bold logo or masthead for your newsletter. You can also use colorful graphics, high-quality illustrations, and vivid photographs. Be sure the print is clear and easy to read.

SENDING MEDIA RELEASES

To be sure, this task is going to take persistence because too often the local newspapers and radio and television stations are more interested in football and basketball, but send them media releases anyway. Provide the information in a news style format and encourage them to attend the next match or tournament.

Keep sending these media releases (see Figure 9-7) whether the information is published or not. Contact these news sources by telephone and try especially to make a friend there. If you can get one reporter or broadcaster on your side, their assistance can do wonders for your program.

You should also invite media personnel to your awards program at the end of the season and write a thank-you letter for the publicity they provided during the season (see Figure 9-8).

DEALING WITH CRITICS AND CRITICISM

Conflict is inevitable whenever large groups of people come together, even if they all are dedicated to the same general goal. No two persons will have identical expectations, interests, or timetables. Every wrestling coach, therefore, should be prepared to confront criticism. An administrator, parent, or wrestler could find fault with his behavior or actions and any form of disapproval can cause even the most confident coach to feel inadequate or uncertain.

This is why you need a system in place that enables you to deal effectively with critics, a system where both sides can feel satisfied with the conflict's resolution. The outcome, in fact, must be constructive, not destructive, and serious effort must be given to solving the problem in a positive way.

Here are ten do's and don't's for dealing with critics and their criticism:

DO'S

1. Do identify as quickly as possible the origin of the dispute.

2. Do display an eagerness to deal with the conflict in a fair and prompt manner.

3. Do take responsibility for solving the problem, without rationalizing any blame on the critic or someone else.

4. Do consider how you have responded to conflicts in the past and accept the responsibility for refining that form of response.

5. Do clarify both sides of the issue before beginning any process of negotiation or compromise.

6. Do learn the background of the critic: What is his/her relationship to you? How much information does he/she have? What other criticisms has he/she delivered in the past?

7. Do remain patient, objective, and understanding, even if the complaint is delivered in an emotional tirade.

8. Do present the critic with the option of working together to solve the problem. If the weight of the criticism can be distributed equally among all involved persons, a strong foundation for improvement is established.

9. Do offer multiple solutions and strategies for dealing with criticism.

10. Do make a public commitment to confronting the criticism and solving the conflict. This leads to a more diligent endeavor on your part in handling it.

DONT'S

1. Do not try to dismiss or deny the criticism. Acknowledge the critic's complaint (possibly accept its validity immediately) and move ahead to its resolution.

2. Do not lose control or allow emotion, especially anger, to cloud your actions. Remain calm and objective, even if the criticism is personal in nature.

3. Do not try to discuss the problem with any person who remains angry or volatile. If hostility emerges, break off any conversation and explain that you will participate again when the other person is more calm.

4. Do not transform the criticism into something greater than it is. If an admiminstrator, for instance, cites your failure to complete paperwork on time, this does not mean you are an incompetent coach.

5. Do not try to make the critic *wrong*. "I'm not wrong, you are!" rarely results in a satisfactory resolution. Instead, make yourself accountable for any mistakes and remain cooperative.

6. Do not withdraw from the issue or ignore it.

7. Do not see any complaint as a challenge to your status as a team leader. Your position as the authority may have nothing to do with the specific criticism.

8. Do not fail to admit to the mistake if the criticism is valid. Recognize the objection being presented about your actions or beliefs as a learning opportunity.

9. Do not repeat the behaviors or actions that originally prompted the criticism.

10. Do not connect another's criticism as a confirmation of any weakness on your part as a coach. It is simply part of the profession. Successful coaches never remain discouraged or indulge in self-pity.

Coaches have to work well within the system and have enough confidence to confront a complaint directly. When they do, their integrity and the school's image are enhanced. One superintendent comments, "Our school is viewed by many only through attendance at athletic contests. The behavior of our athletes, coaches, and fans seriously impacts perceptions about our school district. People should see we are a 'class act.'"

In conclusion, reducing conflicts and minimizing their disruptive influence are crucial to the coaching profession. Keep in mind that conflict leads to both intellectual (solving a problem) and social (building a relationship) growth. Criticism of you or your program should be anticipated and never ignored.

FIGURE 9-1 KEY ASPECTS OF A SUCCESSFUL MEDIA GUIDE

Page 1

Provide:

- Facts about the school—address; phone numbers; nickname SPARTANS; colors BLUE AND WHITE; and enrollment.
- Facts about the school's athletic affiliations—Conference: EAST SUBURBAN CONFERENCE; District or Region: NORTHEAST DISTRICT; Division: DIVISION III; and State: member of OHIO HIGH SCHOOL ATHLETIC ASSOCIATION.
- List of School Administrators—Superintendent, Principal, Assistant Principal(s), Athletic Director, School Board President and Members, and Dean(s) of Students.
- Name of Booster Club President and Officers.
- School Logo.

Page 2

Provide:

- Preview of the coming season.
- Wrestling schedule.

Page 3-4

Profile:

- Head Coach and his background.
- Assistant Coaches, including middle school coaches, and their backgrounds.

Page 5-6

Profile:

- Team roster, beginning with senior wrestlers. Include the pictures of each senior and a photograph of the entire squad.

Page 7-9

List:

- Top career wrestling records;
- The wrestlers selected as the Most Valuable Wrestler through the history of the program;
- The wrestlers selected as team captains through the history of the program;

©1996 by Parker Publishing Company

FIGURE 9-1 CONTINUED

- Top ten record holders in takedowns, pins, near falls, escapes, reversals, and team points;
- Wrestlers who have gone onto compete in college;
- Conference champions—year by year;
- Sectional champions—year by year;
- District champions—year by year;
- Regional placers and champions—year by year;
- Qualifiers to the State Tournament—year by year;
- State placers and champions; and
- Team championships—conference, tournaments, etc.

Page 10

Profile:

- Managers;
- Statisticians;
- Cheerleaders;
- Trainers.

Page 11

Conclude the media guide with an overview of the high school—its academic and other extra-curricular programs (drama, student government, etc.), the composition of its student body, and its reputation for excellence.

You can also provide on a back page some informative details about the sport of wrestling—the scoring, for example—and how wrestlers qualify for the state tournament.

FIGURE 9-2 HISTORICAL/LITERARY ASPECTS OF WRESTLING

KEY FACTS ABOUT WRESTLING

- Most ancient of all sports (15,000 years old based on carvings and drawings found in caves in France).

- Ancient Egyptians and Greeks were deeply involved in the sport of wrestling as wrestling holds have been found on many temples and tombs.

- Part of the ancient Olympiad in 704 BC.

- Earliest recorded match on the Asian continent was in Japan in 22 BC.

- Henry VIII of England wrestled Francis I of France at the Meeting of the Cloth in 1520.

- Legendary figures like Ulysses (Greece) and Jacob (Hebrew) engaged in wrestling matches.

- Essential to the lifestyle of Native Americans prior to the arrival of Columbus.

- George Washington, Abraham Lincoln, and Theodore Roosevelt all earned fame early in their lives as wrestlers.

- Modern wrestling began in the United States after the modern Olympic Games in 1896.

- First intercollegiate meet was held in 1900 between Yale and Penn.

- Famous wrestlers include actor Kirk Douglas; General Norman Schwarzkopf, leader of the Persian Gulf forces; Nobel Prize winning scientist Dr. Norman Borlaug; novelists Ken Kesey (*One Flew Over the Cuckoo's Nest*) and John Irving (*The World According to Garp*); and General George Patton, who led American troops during WW II.

- In the *Illiad,* written by Homer 3000 years ago, a wrestling match between Ajax and Odysseus is described in detail.

FIGURE 9-3 ACADEMIC PROGRESS REPORT

<u>ACADEMIC PROGRESS REPORT—DATE:</u> _____

NAME _____ SUBJECT _____

PLEASE RATE AS SATISFACTORY (S) OR UNSATISFACTORY (U) THIS STUDENT IN THE FOLLOWING CATEGORIES.

RETURN THIS FORM TO COACH _____ EACH FRIDAY. THANK YOU!

S/U   <u>ITEM</u>   <u>COMMENTS</u>

1. ____ ATTITUDE   _____
                                          _____

2. ____ HOMEWORK   _____
                                          _____

3. ____ TESTS/QUIZZES   _____
                                          _____

4. ____ ATTENDANCE   _____
                                          _____

5. ____ PROJECTS   _____
                                          _____

6. CURRENT GRADE   _____

7. OTHER COMMENTS   _____
                                          _____

FIGURE 9-4 THANK YOU LETTER TO COMMUNITY MEMBER

Dear Mr. _____ :

The _____ High School wrestling team is indeed grateful to you for your support of our program. Your generous donation of much needed funds enabled us to purchase Gatorade for use during our tournaments and after our matches.

The coaches and wrestlers truly appreciate your interest and generosity. It is wonderful to recognize that there are many community members like yourself interested in seeing our program succeed. We will certainly commit ourselves to fulfilling the expectations the community has for our wrestling program.

Once again, thank you for your dedicated effort directed toward our wrestling program. It is exciting to see community members support our wrestlers so enthusiastically. We hope to see you attend one or all of our competitions (a schedule is enclosed) and thank you personally.

Gratefully,

The Coaching Staff and Wrestlers of _____ High School

FIGURE 9-5 TYPICAL PARENTS' QUESTIONS FOR WRESTLING COACHES

Parents' Questions About Wrestling

1. **What measures are taken to protect the health of the wrestlers?**

Daily, we stress the use of proper and legal wrestling techniques and manuevers. Coaches monitor closely their actions during all competitive and/or scrimmage wrestling situations so that any risk of an injury is lessened.

Furthermore, the boys are required to wear their headgear during all wrestling and drill sessions to prevent cauliflower ear and other abrasions on the ear or head.

They are also only allowed to wear t-shirts during any drilling and/or wrestling activity instead of a heavy sweatshirt or jersey which could cause dehydration or fatigue to occur too quickly.

Finally, we provide direct access to a trainer, ice, medical kit, and a whirlpool, as needed. If an injury does occur, the coaches contact the parent(s) as soon as possible.

2. **How much weight should my son lose?**

As in many situations, the key concept here is common sense. Your son may not have to lose any weight to wrestle at his weight class. His weight class selection, in fact, should be determined only after he discusses it with both his parents and the coaching staff.

The coaches reject weight loss methods that involve starvation, dehydration, laxatives, induced vomiting, or any other artificial means (saunas, etc.). These methods, in fact, are illegal.

What we hope to accomplish here is a favorable balance between ENERGY IN and ENERGY OUT. When losing weight, you can decrease your calorie intake (ENERGY IN) or increase your physical activity (ENERGY OUT). The most effective approach is a combination of these methods.

Your son should have a well-balanced diet and avoid any "fad" diets which deny him proper nutrition. Moderation is the key in regards to his eating habits—eliminate candy, pastries, junk foods, and snacks between meals. Food portions can be lessened, and you may choose to provide food items high in carbohydrates (pastas, fruit, potatoes, breads) rather than foods high in fat content.

If you believe your son's weight loss methods are wrong or excessive, please contact any coach immediately. If his grades in school suffer or his mood is irritable too often, again contact a coach.

3. **Why do wrestlers choose to lose weight?**

Most wrestlers believe that by dropping excess weight, they can compete in a weight class where they will be stronger. This belief is accurate in most cases,

FIGURE 9-5 CONTINUED

but they must consider their health first. Each wrestler reviews with the coaching staff his percentage of body fat, the number of pounds he wishes to lose, and the level of competition he would face at various weight classes. The coaches are very careful in monitoring each wrestler's weight loss.

4.   How are varsity and junior varsity wrestlers chosen?

Unlike most other sports, positions on the wrestling team are not decided by the coaching staff. Instead, each wrestler competes in a wrestle-off in the practice room against a teammate(s) to determine the varsity competitor. Another name for this is challenge matches.

After the winning wrestler has earned his position on the varsity, the remaining competitors at his weight class become starters on the junior varsity or freshmen team.

However, the coaching staff retains the right to name the varsity wrestler at each weight class as circumstances dictate—injury, discipline, experience—for each dual meet.

5.   What do they do at practice?

Each practice session begins with a comprehensive warm up, followed by agility drills, running or weightlifting, and "buddy" drills where boys practice the same maneuver or technique with a partner under the guidance of the coaching staff. Much repitition is necessary here.

Each day, a coach or clinician teaches a new skill or technique, which is then drilled until it is mastered.

Final elements of a typical practice are competitive wrestling, where the boys are expected to compete against each other intensely and aggressively, and a conditioning session, which often involves an aerobic workout.

6.   What kind of physical changes should I expect to observe in my son?

First, since most wrestlers choose to lose at least some weight over the season, you may notice that their pants fit more loosely, their faces become more taut, and their upper body begins to show more muscle definition. Their endurance and stamina levels increase, and they become more flexible due to the exercises performed during practices.

On the down side, you may also notice bumps and bruises form on their cheeks, legs, and arms. These are typical areas that come in contact with an opponent or drill partner, so some type of a black-and-blue spot can be expected occasionally. He should also demonstrate more fatigue during the week since he is working very hard for five or six straight days.

FIGURE 9-5 CONTINUED

7. **What kind of psychological changes should I expect to observe in my son?**

He may become more irritable and moody. Wrestling is a long season where for two-and-a-half hours every day the boys sweat and strain in an enclosed area, pounding on each other to prepare for the next competition. That competition involves a one-on-one situation that can make even the most poised person nervous. Therefore, it is crucial that parents work to keep their son's spirits as high as possible.

Please contact a coach immediately if your son's moody behavior turns into belligerence. This should not be tolerated regardless of any anxiety he may be feeling.

8. **What should I do if there is a problem?**

We ask that all major problems be directed as soon as possible to the head coach. However, for minor problems or concerns, feel free to discuss them with the coach you find most accessible. Call the school or the head coach at home if any matter needs to be addressed.

FIGURE 9-6 SAMPLE NEWSLETTER

RICHMOND HEIGHTS WRESTLING—1989

Head Coach: Keith Manos
Asst. Coach: Larry Hauserman
447 Richmond Road
Richmond Heights, OH 44143
(216) 692-0094

SPARTAN NEWS

Our kids made us proud, didn't they? Every fan of the Spartans should recognize the accomplishments of the outstanding performers on this team. Our kids competed aggressively and earned a lot of respect, whether they won or lost. Regardless of the outcome, we saw champions in action every time.

TEAM RESULTS

- East Suburban Conference Champions (undefeated at 7-0)
- Sectional Tournament Runner-up (out of 12 teams)
- District Tournament Champions (out of 54 teams)
- 3rd in Division III State Tournament
- United Press International Poll Champions in Division III
- 14-0 Dual Meet Season

INDIVIDUAL TOURNAMENT RESULTS

	1st	*2nd*	*3rd*	*4th*
Sectional:	Wrestler's Name Names	Wrestler's Name Names	Wrestler's Name Names	Names
District:	Names	Names	Names	Names
State:	Names	Names	Names	Names

FINAL VARSITY STATISTICS

WT/NAME	RECORD	TD	ESC	REV	NF	PINS	TOTAL PTS
103 NAME	15-5	30	13	8	24	4	65
112 NAME	20-6	36	24	12	19	8	96
119 NAME	14-13	28	25	5	7	3	42
125 NAME	31-2	99	16	9	29	8	163
130 NAME	16-6	51	23	7	19	7	76
135 NAME	24-1	63	12	12	45	8	146
140 NAME	32-5	88	22	9	34	8	147

FIGURE 9-6 CONTINUED

WT/NAME	RECORD	TD	ESC	REV	NF	PINS	TOTAL PTS
145 NAME	11-6	21	8	2	10	2	41
152 NAME	25-5	46	18	7	40	11	149
160 NAME	26-4	93	22	5	22	5	150
171 NAME	12-7	13	7	8	17	3	43
189 NAME	15-10	35	17	10	7	2	59
HWT NAME	2-12	2	5	2	1	1	12

SPECIAL ANNOUNCEMENTS

- Winter Sports Awards Program

  When: Wed., March 29 at 7:30 P.M.
  Where: High School Auditorium
  What: Awarding of Varsity and Junior Varsity letters and Special
            Awards Trophies

SPECIAL THANK YOU'S

- To Mr. _____ for videotaping all our dual meets

- To Mr. and Mrs. _____ for the wonderful victory party after our final dual meet. The kids had a great time, and the coaches appreciate your efforts.

- To Mrs. _____ for all the photographs you took of our wrestlers this season.

- To the Booster Club for their continued support and donation of t-shirts to our conference champion team.

- To Mr. and Mrs. _____ for hosting the boys in between the sessions of the District Tournament. We're grateful for the spaghetti and the time we could relax in your home.

- To Mrs. _____ , advisor for the Mat Stats, for the excellent job our girls do scoring at every competition.

- To Mr. _____ , athletic director, for his continued support through the season.

- To the school administration for their efforts in supporting the program and granting all our requests.

END QUOTES

"A total commitment is paramount in reaching the ultimate in performance. You should always stand tall and proud when you have given your best." (from Tom Flores, NFL Coach)

"We grow by great dreams. All big men are dreamers." (from Woodrow Wilson, 28th President)

FIGURE 9-7 MEDIA RELEASE

Sample Media Release

To _____ Date _____

From Head Wrestling Coach _____

Re: Richmond Heights Invitational Wrestling Tournament Placers

The Richmond Hts. High School Spartans won the team championship trophy at their own invitational tournament ahead of a field of 16 teams on Saturday, Dec. ___, 19 ___.

The following wrestlers achieved placement:

Brian Smith (103)—Champion

Bill Smith (119)—Runner up

Matt Musarra (125)—Runner up

Mike Connely (135)—Fourth Place

Herb Adkins (140)—Champion

Pat Campolieti (145)—Champion

Joe Daugherty (152)—Third Place

Greg Leinweber (171)—Champion

Dan Agresta (HWT)—Fourth Place

The Spartan's current dual meet record is 5-1 and competes next in a quad match at Beachwood High School on Dec. ___, 19 ____.

For further information call _____ anytime between _____.

FIGURE 9-8 THANK YOU LETTER TO THE MEDIA

Dear _____

Your coverage of our dual meet against _____ High School effectively described the competitive effort put forth by both teams. It was an exciting match, and all the athletes, coaches, and parents associated with our program are grateful you reported on it.

We are especially pleased that you highlighted several individual performances. Overall, your article was informative and entertaining. Our parents, students, and staff look forward to reading more like it.

Again, thanks for the recent article and your continued coverage of _____ wrestling.

With appreciation,

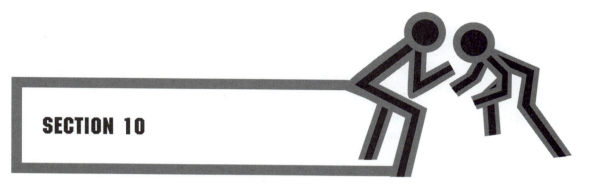

SECTION 10

Our Changing Profession

In the 1950's, the coach was loved by administrators, respected by kids, and adored by parents. He was the General Schwarzkopf of the school, strutting down hallways as if inspecting the troops. Athletes tensed beneath his anger after any loss and dumped him in the showers after that championship victory.

Maybe your coach was a gray-haired legend, or a soft-spoken saint, or the only respected authority in the school. You might even have tried to adopt his persona with your own teams, but in truth there aren't many of these kinds of coaches (in any sport) today. Furthermore, any form of adoration is rare. Frank Romano, assistant wrestling coach at Kent State University and a coaching veteran of 24 years, laments that the celebrity status of coaching is gone. "Things have changed," he says. "We're peons now."

If the wrestling coaches before 1970 were heroes, what has happened in twenty years to change that image?

THE LEADERSHIP CRISIS

"The coach was everything in the 1960's," Don Wem recalls. Wem has coached football, soccer, wrestling, and track for nearly thirty years at several Ohio schools. "Now," he adds, "kids feel the coach can't tell them that much. They just don't care." Many of Wem's colleagues, who feel threatened by the changing environment of sports and the less diligent habits of the athletes, agree. The uncertainty they have about dealing with their athletes often surfaces in the indecisive way they manage their teams.

Usually, inexperience is the key factor behind a coach's inability to provide satisfactory leadership. Indeed, fewer individuals are in fact interested in coaching, and many of those that do coach become so overwhelmed and exhausted by the many duties forced on them that they quit after their first year. This is especially true in wrestling where enthusiasm at the beginning of a season can often lead to frustration at its end for these coaches. Consequently, they choose to terminate their coaching careers before they even get started. School administrators then confront again the difficulty of locating and training a new coach for the team.

Gary Walton, whose research about the coaching profession appears in his book *Beyond Winning*, understands the administrator's dilemma. "People attracted to these important positions today bring a different array of skills. The importance of leadership and education still exists, but other roles compete for the scarce time available, and there is less time for a coach to provide personal direction to student athletes. And the stress is causing an alarming number of coaches to depart the profession early."

Stress weakens effectiveness. Every week of any typical season, coaches can experience tension caused by conflicts with unfocused wrestlers and antagonistic parents. Even a coach's own competitive attitude can lead to anxiety as he pushes himself to win matches. In this kind of domain, disagreements are common, and confrontations are frequent. If they are not handled effectively, it is possible that the coach's composure can collapse and his self-esteem suffer.

When coaches fail to manage these situations properly, they exhibit symptoms associated with poor leadership: doubt, anger, frustration, negativity, regrets, and even poor health. They leave conflicts unresolved and sometimes over-react to challenges. If they can eliminate their own self-destructive behaviors and emotional surges, they can become better coaches.

A variety of factors are changing the coaching profession: Advancements in technology, the unstable character or performance of many athletes, and the aggressive presence of the media are all contributing to this transformation. "These forces are pulling the modern head coach in directions different in both scope and intensity than coaches of earlier generations," says Walton.

Coaches must be especially attentive the way they treat their wrestlers during practices and matches, especially after a loss. Many of today's coaches may have grown up in an era where their coaches used discipline and punishment to motivate wrestlers, but that style is rarely tolerated today (Bobby Knight is a major exception). According to William Beausay, president of the Academy of Sports Psychology International in Columbus, Ohio, coaches who intimidate or threaten athletes should not be allowed to continue coaching. Beausay also points out that today's young athletes won't tolerate abusive coaches because they are much more independent than their counterparts in previous decades.

When coaches physically or mentally abuse their athletes, their behavior "borders on pathological," says Frank Smoll, a professor of psychology at the University of Washington. Smoll feels that the more effective coaches utilize a liberal amount of rewards, reinforcements, and praise as opposed to those who lean toward punitive measures to influence their players' performances.

The whole coaching profession is often criticized for the actions of those few who perform their duties in childish ways. Ron Fimrite, noted columnist for *Sports Illustrated*, believes that those coaches who behave publicly without dignity or respectability may be doing so because "we have come to accept childishness as a kind of virtue in sports. We seem to have, clutching desperately to the helms, a sorry collection of aging juveniles who are about as qualified to direct and inspire young people as was old Fagin himself." Fimrite notes that another root to the problem is the coach's aggressiveness, like the kind exhibited by the late Billy Martin and Woody Hayes.

Fimrite's solution? He recommends that school officials stop compensating and applauding the coach who "behaves like a perfect fool and not only gets away with it but also is . . . rewarded with a position of authority."

In contrast to the type of coach described by Fimrite is Ladd Holman, the head wrestling coach at Delta High School in Utah, whose teams have won 23 state titles. His formula for success involves following a sequence of steps: Set a specific goal; decide what needs to be sacrificed to reach the goal; and work hard enough to achieve the goal. Ladd also instructs his wrestlers "to stay humble out there after a win or a loss. We always want a class act because everyone is watching us. I would rather work with a wrestler who is willing to work and has character than one who simply has talent."

If we coaches are to improve our image and revitalize our profession, we can't become dismayed or discouraged by the problems cited by Walton or Fimrite. Perserverence, patience, and better public relations are needed to deal with these issues, and we should also reconsider how autocratic or democratic we wish to be with our wrestling teams. Wrestlers truly have changed, and the more successful coaches have changed with them.

To be sure, criticism of the coaching profession will always exist, and no coach escapes some form of disapproval during his career. Yet, with effort, every coach can transform this negative energy into a more positive, productive force and emerge as a confident leader. This kind of coach affirms his position as a capable authority figure by:

- ☑ anticipating problems before they reach the crisis stage;

- ☑ maintaining a professional demeanor although others may be dominated by their emotions;

- ☑ remaining assertive but not confrontational when dealing with opposing points of view;

- ☑ repairing damaged relationships through compromise and cooperation;

- ☑ recognizing the differences between healthy and harmful anger in his wrestlers and himself and how to channel this emotion into an emotional force;

- ☑ confronting difficult people and situations directly without being intimidated or provoked;

- ☑ being regularly accessible for others when a problem comes up;

- ☑ communicating in an honest, straightforward way with others;

- ☑ establishing himself as a person to be trusted and respected; and

- ☑ refusing to let any kind of criticism ruin his ego or effectiveness as a coach.

THE STATE OF SPORTSMANSHIP

Robert Kanaby, executive director of the National Federation of State High School Associations, reveals that the biggest challenge facing athletic programs across the country this decade is the type of education athletes experience with their coaches. Increasing student involvement is important, Kanaby says, but the "promotion of sportsmanship, the teaching of values, ethical behavior and acting with integrity must be at the top of our list." The NFSHSA's top priority "is to eliminate unsportsmanlike behavior, but the reality is that we're going to have to continue to deal with it, not only year by year, but game by game."

Sportsmanship, too, seems to be slowly disappearing from the sports scene. Watch any professional football, basketball, or hockey game and you'll witness combative players, belligerent coaches, and unruly spectators. "We're not just devoid of sportsmanship," says Tom Tutko, psychology professor at San Jose State University and keynote speaker for a National Youth Sports Coaches Association summit meeting, "we're anti-sportsmanship." Tutko points to an increase in the occurrence of violence, drugs, and neurotic behavior among athletes and coaches.

Consider the following examples:

—More than 100 boys in Ohio were ejected from high school and junior high soccer games during the first two weeks of the 1994 season, according to the Ohio High School Athletic Association.

—According to a national poll conducted by ESPN, 80 percent of the people responded that there was less sportsmanship displayed today than ten years ago.

—After getting pinned, an Ohio wrestler got in the face of his opponent, voiced several obscenities, and raised his fists, claiming that he would have won had it been "a street fight."

—The eight schools in the Marmonte League in California voted unanimously in 1994 to abandon any post-game handshake between players in all sports because it was "not really the symbol of sportsmanship it is purported to be and . . . it carries a risk" of potential violence.

Frank Martin, who serves as the executive director of the NYSCA's Texas chapter admits that he wasn't surprised when he learned that players and parents staged a mini-riot at a little league baseball game in Albuquerque. "A lot of coaches will walk in with the mistaken idea that the way they coach on television is the way that youth leagues should be run as well."

Citing the increase in athletes taunting each other, being ejected from matches, and leaving the bench to join a fight, Hank Zaborniak, director of officiating for the Ohio High School Athletic Association, sees sportsmanship "on a steady decline."

Harry Edwards, Professor of Sociology at the University of California at Berkeley, states, "If abolishing niceties such as handshakes at the end of games is needed to preserve high school sports, then it should be done without regret." Zaborniak adds: "If we're not going to be teaching people skills and values for the rest of their lives, what are we doing? One thing all kids have to learn is that things aren't always going to go right. You win with grace, and you lose with grace."

Coaches can have a major impact on their athlete's understanding of sportsmanship: They must not only promote but also model themselves honest, ethical behavior even at the expense of fulfilling their own self-interests. Wrestlers must be taught to see wrestling as one of the fairest sports since it provides equal opportunity for participation regardless of size, race, or age.

Sportsmanship should surface especially in the one-on-one format of a wrestling competition where a wrestler, competing against an opponent of identical weight, has a fair chance to gain a victory. His parents should be taught to respect each wrestler's hard work to prepare for that competition and applaud their efforts in the match, regardless of its outcome. Everyone has to realize that success is cheapened when sporstmanship is violated.

THE ATHLETE AND HIS ACADEMICS

Eligibility must certainly be a major concern for most coaches. We all recognize that the wrestler's performance in the classroom is much more important than his results on the mat. Therefore, you should be especially attentive to each wrestler's academic standing—assisting those with tutoring or time off who are having difficulties and rewarding those who are earning high grades.

You might also consider setting up a "Study Table" where wrestlers gather before practice to complete homework or review for tests. A weekly or bi-weekly progress report (see Figure 9-3) could be arranged for any wrestler you believe is doing poorly in the classroom. If problems (low grades, missing assignments, etc.) do occur, you can respond to them promptly with a tutoring session or time off from practice.

CLIPBOARDS AND COMPUTERS

Coaching is obviously more than a practice plan attached to a clipboard or statistics punched into a computer. A coach must display loyalty to his school, friendship to his wrestlers, and integrity towards opponents. He must have a highly developed conscience and the courage to take a stand. Coaching a wrestling team is not an obligation, it is an opportunity to contribute to an athlete's life.

The ability to organize a practice and operate a computer enhance a coach's training, but personal qualities cannot be ignored. Compassion, patience, honesty, persistence, commitment—these are the traits that the best coaches possess.

Vince Dooley, athletic director at the University of Georgia, advises coaches about the importance of making a sincere commitment. "After you have made a commitment, you must keep your mind open to new ideas and learn from your experiences with players and coaches. Coaching is a continuous educational process, and you must learn from everyone around you." In fact, the coach must look upon each season as a learning experience.

*"Some coaches are so busy learning the tricks
of the trade that they never learn the trade."*

—(FROM PETE EMELIANCHIK, NEW YORK CITY JUNIOR HIGH COACH)

THE BUDGET, FUND RAISING, AND "PAY TO PLAY"

In many school districts it takes a lot of money for kids to participate in sports, and if a school district faces a financial hardship, the first place they look to cut funds is the athletic department. Because of this in many parts of the country "pay to play" has been instituted by school boards who hope to compensate for the high cost of operating their athletic programs.

A lower budget for the athletic department means your sport suffers also. According to former athletic director Mike Papouras, who logged over 16 years at that position, heavy restrictions on uniform and equipment purchases needed to be written into the athletic department handbook. Once a wrestling coach himself, Papouras regretted imposing these restrictions on his coaches, yet the action was necessary. The funds simply weren't there. He regrets with greater feeling the school's strong dependency on its booster club for money. "My palm was always out," he remembers. I'd feel like a beggar." Coaches need to recognize the influence of "the bottom line" on today's administrators, athletes, and parents.

Along with the growing popularity of "pay to play" in secondary schools, there is the real threat of school boards eliminating high school sports if voters do not pass a tax levy for the school. Ohio High School Athletic Association Assistant Commisioner Duane Warns observes: "We're seeing school districts trying to use athletics as a club to pass levies because many people consider athletics to be high priority. We have seen a lot of Ohio school boards choosing this option to pass their levies."

"Whether you like it or not, cutting extra-curriculars gets the attention of the voting public," says Bill Borland, Athletic Director at Urbana High School in Ohio.

Plan your wrestling budget and any fund-raising efforts carefully. An administrator from a highly successful athletic program in California reports that "budgets may cover tournament fees, but not much more. Coaches must raise the funds for uniforms and anything else they desire for the program." A New Jersey athletic director remains worried about the decreasing amount of funds provided by the state government: "The athletic programs will feel it first. I'm afraid the future holds less, not more, for athletics."

To add funds to your wrestling budget, you have several options:

1. Initiate your own fund raiser with the approval of the administration.

2. Institute a "pay-to-play" policy, which could make each athlete obligated to pay a fee ($10-100.00) per sport. A fee of fifty dollars is the national average.

3. Obtain corporate sponsorship.

4. Seek donations from local businesses.

5. Sell old uniforms, warm-ups, or mats.

6. Host a wrestling tournament in the spring or summer where you charge an entry fee ($10) but use volunteer table workers and officials.

7. Form a "Wrestling Booster Club" that can organize fund raising projects—raffles, concession stand, auctions.

8. Improve the competitiveness of your program to increase attendance at home dual meets and money gained through ticket sales.

Regarding your budget, you should consider allocating funds for the following items that typically are essential for any wrestling program:

1. fees paid to officials, table workers, announcers, scorers, or mat movers;

2. fees paid to trainers and/or other medical personnel;

3. funds required for travel, mileage, and lodging (tournaments);

4. registration fees for clinics or meetings;

5. funds available for meals and beverages (at tournaments and after weigh-ins);

6. purchases of equipment (headgear), uniforms, warm-ups, or knee pads;

7. dues and entry fees for invitational tournaments and state sponsored tournaments; and

8. funds for photography, mailing, printing, or office equipment.

THE ATHLETE OF THE '90S

Key Point #1—Research Your Athletes

"I think to be effective you have to really know your athletes and be able to adapt to the situation to fit the need of each athlete," says one Ohio college coach. "Everyone is a little different, and I like seeing how far they can progress." To build a solid foundation for your program you should first find out what kind of kids are walking the hallways of your school. Are sports important to them? Does competition excite them? Can they commit themselves to the strenuous wrestling practices?

You need to do some research about the athletes in your school. One way is to have informal discussions where you ask each one about his interests and background. This is, of course, a more personal and time-consuming way of discovering information, but it often leads to a closer relationship between you and each wrestler, which is important if you are going to spend a lot of time together.

Another way to learn more about athletes in your school is to have them complete a brief questionnaire (see Figure 10-1) in their homerooms. This survey identifies for the coach an athlete's perceptions of athletic achievement. Do they consider talent more important that attitude, strength more essential than hard work? The results provide a coach with insights into the athlete's view of his own potential to succeed in sports (wrestling).

A coach can obtain a more comprehensive psychological profile of each wrestler with a competitive behavior questionnaire (see Figure 10-2). Results here enable a coach to discern in detail a wrestler's mental approach to competition and eliminate any anxieties he may have.

Key Point #2—Share Athletes in the School

According to Jeffrey Saks, who has covered high school sports for several Ohio newspapers, "the three-sport athlete is a dinosaur, and even two-sport athletes soon may follow them to extinction . . . Coaches who want their teams to win demand more and more out of their athletes."

Jim Reed has coached at Liberty Union High School in Ohio for 27 years, and he is dismayed by a growing trend of coaches who demand too much of the athletes' time in order to win. "In between seasons, kids have very little time to recover, and I'm not just talking about physical recovery . . . You put yourself in a position sometimes of going downhill without any brakes. But I still say the coach has the option to draw some lines."

Another veteran Ohio coach recognizes the strong need for coaches to cooperate with sharing athletes, even in the larger schools. "I think it's really important that the coaches all understand about the kids' time needs. I'd hate to be in a situation where one coach was pulling a player one way and another was pulling a player another way."

A major issue for coaches of the 1990's is whether or not they should encourage their athletes to specialize in one sport. With open tournaments and technique clinics available almost year round, wrestlers are directly affected by this issue.

"It's one of those things where I don't know if I'm for it or against it," admits one coach. "I know everyone else is doing something, so you feel like you have to. But it's screwed up my summer and my kids' summer."

Lancaster High School coach Lennie Conrad realizes that college recruiters are interested in athletes who can perform in several sports. "That's what they want to know, what he can do in other sports. They want to know whether the kid will compete. That's the real reason for playing more than one sport, keeping your competitive edge."

Should athletes specialize? It certainly is an important discussion that coaches in every school need to have early in the school year. There should be no misunderstandings and no hard feelings between them. Most importantly, the individual needs of the athletes need to be addressed. Sharing becomes even more crucial at smaller schools where fewer talented athletes are available.

Another veteran coach adds: "I think the ones who are multiple-sport participants are more dedicated, and they train year round, and you don't have the problems at the beginning of the season with soreness. I like for my athletes to play more than one sport."

"We'd rather the student-athlete not specialize," says OHSAA commissioner Clair Muscaro. "I don't think specialization is good. We'd like to see them involved in as many sports as possible."

There are several arguments against specialization:

☑ It can deprive some teams of athletes and put smaller programs at risk.

☑ It could deny a younger athlete the opportunity to participate in another sport where he has a greater potential for success.

☑ It contradicts most school's advocacy of developing a student's proficiency in many areas.

☑ It promotes rivalries between coaches in a school system, resulting in conflicts and hurt feelings with the athlete caught in the middle.

Obviously, cooperation between the coaching staff is crucial when an athlete(s) considers specializing in a single sport. No coach should push an athlete into focusing on one sport, nor punish him if he doesn't specialize. An excellent example against specialization is Southeast High School in Lincoln, Nebraska, which has won at least one state championship for 20 straight years. Athletic director Larry Munksgaard says, "The cooperative feeling among coaches is unique. They are constantly encouraging their athletes to go out for other sports. The coaches are team players themselves."

Key Point #3—Teach Effective Weight Loss

One of our sport's major public relations problems is the issue of weight loss. We get complaints from mothers and warnings from physicians whenever a wrestler chooses to compete at a weight class lower than his present weight. But this is a part of wrestling you must be ready to deal with.

Surveys have shown that most boys learn how to lose weight from a teammate and refuse to consult a physician who, they believe, does not understand the sport or its pressures. It becomes, therefore, up to the coach to advise each athlete about the lowest weight at which he can compete successfully and the appropriate methods he can use to make that weight class (see Figures 10-3 and 10-4).

Though most healthy, active boys can lose a number of pounds without harming their health or stamina, never encourage or force their decision to compete at a weight class. If you do, then their making weight becomes your responsibility and not theirs. The parents need to be informed from the beginning about their son's weight class selection, and their approval must be granted.

At times you may have to discourage weight loss especially if you notice a wrestler's performing poorly at his studies and on the wrestling mat. If he's frequently sluggish, irritable, and tense you should re-evaluate either the weight classification where he competes or the methods he's using to make that weight class.

Effective weight loss for wrestlers depends on:

1. monitoring the calories they consume each day;

2. avoiding unsafe weightloss methods like diuretics or laxatives;

3. eliminating the binge-starvation cycle that too many wrestlers use to make weight (this leaves them more fatigued in competition);

4. sustaining muscles with an ample supply of water;

5. consuming carbohydrates and fruits in proper amounts (this includes bananas, apples, corn, breads, pasta, potatoes, noodles, and rice);

6. building and retaining glycogen in the muscles by eating these carbohydrates and replacing water lost through sweat;

7. avoiding "fad" diets and diet pills;

8. calculating their body fat at the beginning of the season to determine their safest margin of weight loss (no wrestler should attempt to lose more than 8 percent of his body weight, and anyone with a body fat measurement of 7 percent or less should not lose any weight);

9. beginning weight loss early, before the competitive season begins, and progressing slowly, dropping 1-3 pounds per week; and

10. weighing in before and after every practice session.

It would be wise for coaches to provide pre-match meals for their wrestlers as often as possible. Depending on the duration of time between the weigh-in and the match time, wrestlers can consume safely any of the following foods: bagels, waffles or pancakes without syrup, fresh fruit, fruit yogurt, raisins, dates, fig bars, lemonade, soup, granola, toast, tea, honey, or a sport drink.

Key Point #4—Avoid Skin Diseases

Currently, the sport of wrestling suffers from an epidemic of skin diseases and the threat of infection by the HIV virus. Even the Environmental Protection Agency has responded to the matter by recommending that coaches promote proper hygiene practices to their athletes on a daily basis.

More distressing are the rumors that wrestling should no longer be a sanctioned sport since the close contact of the competitors for six minutes places each one in jeopardy of contracting the dreaded HIV virus. Though there is no documented case of an athlete contracting the HIV virus at the amateur or professional level during a contest, athletes, coaches, and parents are concerned. "This is such a controversial subject," says Urbana High School wrestling coach Jack Beard, "you have to go with your personal beliefs. If I thought you could contract AIDS through wrestling, I wouldn't coach. And I would never put these kids in jeopardy."

Ohio High School Athletic Association commissioner Debbie Moore dismisses the rumors vehemently. "The risk is very minimal and any rumored cases of HIV contraction from athletic competition have not been substantiated. The chance of contracting HIV is slim in the athletic setting." Moore, however, does acknowledge the importance of coaches following the guidelines developed by the NCAA and the National Federation of State Athletic Associations:

1. Wear latex gloves whenever exposed to mucous membranes or body fluids.

2. Wash hands and any contaminated skin immediately after touching body fluids.

3. Have athletes change uniforms when they become contaminated with any body fluid.

4. Disinfect with bleach, Lysol, or a special iodine solution all surfaces (wrestling mats) that are exposed to body fluids.

5. Warn athletes about the dangers of engaging in unprotected sexual relations (the 13-19-year-old age group is the fastest-growing segment of the the AIDS-infected population).

Ohio Physical Therapy and Sports Medicine, Inc. offers the following recommendations:

1. Make wrestlers shower after every practice and match, including after each match in a tournament.

2. Disinfect headgears, floor mats, wall mats, and the school showers each day.

3. Have a special pathogen kit available to clean up blood on a wrestler's skin.

4. Provide antibacterial soaps, like Safeguard, for wrestlers.

5. Disinfect wrestling shoes and travel bags once a week.

6. Be sure wrestlers are having their practice gear and clothing cleaned daily.

Whenever confronted by a questionable skin condition on a wrestler, coaches should refer him immediately to a medical doctor or dermatologist for diagnosis. They should also familiarize themselves with skin rashes like herpes, impetigo, scabies, and ringworm to be able to make this referral more promptly. "Coaches have to do all they can to ensure the health of their athletes," Beard advises. "You can clean the mats every day and do all you're supposed to do, but over the years . . . there's still no guarantee some infections won't occur."

Key Point #5—Become a Role Model

Walton in the introduction to his book *Beyond Winning* likens today's coaches "to the ancient philosopher kings." To a junior athlete at a Cleveland high school, the

coach was an "inspiration. He inspired me to be the best I could be and never give up."
To Marc Pedmo, an all star football player and state tournament wrestler, the
wrestling coach "was like a father . . . He was very understanding and sincere, and I
knew he would go out on a limb for me."

These are the expectations people have of coaches. Once you decide to coach, you
become a role model. Coaches are always in a position to model the proper behavior
and actions that most members of society respect and admire. As role models, coaches are expected to:

1. be outstanding teachers;

2. have great knowledge of the sport;

3. communicate effectively;

4. develop athletes' skills and talents;

5. teach morals, ethics, and a team concept;

6. prepare kids for the rigors of life;

7. discipline the athletes fairly and consistently;

8. influence athletes to attend college;

9. empathize with kids' problems;

10. reflect a positive attitude;

11. establish a good rapport with the athletes;

12. be patient and understanding;

13. have a sense of humor;

14. develop school and team spirit;

15. remain committed and dedicated to the team;

16. be enthusiastic and motivated;

17. strive to be successful and competitive;

18. organize successfully the entire program;

19. cooperate with the entire coaching staff; and

20. be a friend to athletes.

Once coaches accept these responsibilities they are more likely to build the self-
esteem and physical skills of their wrestlers. The wrestlers and the general public
will come to admire coaches for their commitment, sincerity, knowledge, and enthusiasm. They also will enjoy a loyal following. Ryan Massey, a middle school wrestler,
has a more simple criteria for determining a coach who is an effective role model:
"They have to be funny and cool and like cartoons."

THE FUTURE FOR A WRESTLING COACH

Consider the following:

—In Hollidaysburg, Pennsylvania, school officials drop the requirement that high school students take showers after physical education classes after the American Civil Liberties Union threatens to sue.

—A dual meet to determine the conference champion is cancelled when a brawl erupts between the two teams. The head coach of one of the teams eventually is taken to court for inciting a riot.

—The finals of a tournament are suspended while police and officials break up a fight between the mother and father of opposing wrestlers.

—In Minnesota, several students who changed schools to improve their athletic status committed suicide when their performances didn't match the expectations. To be sure, these suicides have not been linked to the change in environment, yet the pressure to perform beyond their actual abilities cannot be ignored as a contributing factor.

Whether you expect problems like this to diminish or worsen in the coming year, they are part of the climate that surrounds a wrestling coach. The coach's eyes must be opened wide to function in this domain, which is inherently based on conflict. You must be a special person who is prepared to address complex issues like violence, litigation, and AIDS while trying to produce competitive teams. Our predecessors rarely worried about any of these things.

Overall, wrestlers today are more talented and experienced, and their interest in winning matches is as strong as it ever was. But keep in mind that they are also working in the same difficult and sometimes dangerous environment you are.

Coaches have to analyze their wrestlers' parents who may view their son's participation in wrestling in a variety of ways. Sometimes, parents simply want the coach to be a babysitter for them while others are ready to identify even minor mistakes. One parent says, "I try not to be vocal in my criticism of the coach. It's just that some coaches get too close to the athletes, too intense, and lose all their objectivity and fairness. Coaches have to keep a distance."

A coach could feel threatened or intimidated by a comment like this, but a parent never begins as an adversary. Coaches who are fair, competent, and caring rarely receive complaints from parents. If they treat their wrestlers with respect and promote self-discipline, they easily earn the support of parents.

"I expect my son's coach to teach him good technique, make him work, make clear what he's doing right and wrong, but never abuse him," says David Hill, a professor of philosophy at Augustana College. "I know my son will come to understand about differences in ability and learn to lose, but I'm also concerned that the coach has a sensible overall perspective."

You probably will struggle with the disappointment associated with failing to win matches and to accomplish goals. Maybe you will confront a low salary given by the school board and the poor behavior exhibited by the wrestlers. You may leave practice exhausted, maybe even injured. Yet, all these things are part of the profession.

Robert Kanaby warns that "if anything is going to destroy high school sports in this country, it's going to be that people will believe sports have lost their educational purpose . . . You just don't walk away when the game is won or lost. There's a responsibility that carries itself into the locker room, into the school bus, and right on down the line."

Jerry Kramer, the former offensive lineman for the Green Bay Packers, understands the coach's situation: "We must pay a price for success. It's like anything worthwhile. It has a price. You have to pay the price to win and you have to pay the price to get to the point where success is possible."

If you are currently coaching, the thought of resigning has probably crossed your mind several times. If so, follow these recommendations. Stop coaching only when:

☑ the fun is gone;

☑ the hours seem too long;

☑ when tying the shoe laces of your wrestling shoes is too difficult;

☑ you become too fatigued too quickly;

☑ you're leaving education for another line of work;

☑ you become a school administrator;

☑ you complain too often about your supplemental contract or the kids you coach; and/or

☑ the challenge is gone because all the goals you set for yourself are accomplished.

Ben Peterson offers a special tribute to the sport of wrestling and the men who coach it: "Wrestling cannot change the nature of man, but it can bring out the qualities that are intended to lead others, encourage others, challenge others, entertain others, and direct others. I am thankful to God for the sport of wrestling and its maturing effects in the lives of many young men."

Coaching under any conditions in today's schools can be a worthwhile and enjoyable experience. If you have stamina and enthusiasm, you can have a rewarding career. You don't have to win championships right away, and kids most often will forgive you for your errors if you forgive them for theirs.

Coaching is a way to contribute to young people's lives. Few adults in their lives help them set goals, train them to achieve those objectives, and then reward them for their efforts. Wrestling especially offers athletes a wonderful opportunity for physical, mental, and social growth. You are the catalyst for this growth.

It certainly can be a demanding, sometimes thankless, task to take on the responsibility of coaching another adult's child. Many coaches question that decision on a daily basis until they hear just a single statement of gratitude from an athlete on their team.

A coach's influence can have a tremendous impact on the life of an athlete. Today, more and more kids would follow a path towards alcohol, drugs, and gangs if not for a coach guiding them in a more positive direction. Clearly, there's a lot at stake when you choose to coach wrestling, and there is a lot to accomplish. I hope this is a challenge that appeals to you. It does to me.

FIGURE 10-1 ANALYZING SUCCESS IN ATHLETICS

What does it take to be a successful athlete?

Please rate from 1-15 with 15 being the most important item and 1 being the least important the following items in regards to being a successful athlete:

_____ Dedication and determination

_____ Strength

_____ Ability to concentrate

_____ Flexibility

_____ Good positive mental attitude

_____ Talent

_____ Intelligence

_____ Confidence

_____ Competitve drive

_____ Quickness and mobility

_____ Good physical conditioning

_____ Liking the sport (enthusiasm)

_____ Ability to cooperate with others

_____ Coordination and agility

_____ Self-motivation

FIGURE 10-2 COMPETITIVE BEHAVIOR QUESTIONNAIRE

Name _____ Date _____

How Competitive Are You?

Circle the number under the choice that best describes you, being sure to respond truthfully to each statement.

	Statement	Always	Sometimes	Never
1.	I get nervous when people watch me compete.	3	2	1
2.	Before a contest I have trouble sleeping.	3	2	1
3.	I can't focus after making a mistake.	3	2	1
4.	I perform better in practice than a match.	3	2	1
5.	I make more mistakes when the score is close.	3	2	1
6.	I get angry at myself when I make mistakes in a competition.	3	2	1
7.	I am a "clutch" player when the pressure is on.	3	2	1
8.	When a coach yells I lose my focus.	3	2	1
9.	I stay focused and positive before any competition.	3	2	1
10.	I get easily distracted before a contest.	3	2	1
11.	The more challenging the competition the better I perform.	3	2	1
12.	I enjoy competing.	3	2	1
13.	I don't like to think about the contest because it makes me too nervous.	3	2	1
14.	I worry a lot about getting injured.	3	2	1
15.	I usually feel sick or weak before a contest.	3	2	1
16.	I set my own goals for practice and contests.	3	2	1
17.	I rarely listen to my coach during a contest.	3	2	1
18.	I perform best when I'm nervous or worried.	3	2	1
19.	I always compete up to my potential.	3	2	1
20.	I'm usually disappointed by the outcomes of my competitions.	3	2	1
21.	The butterflies bother me throughout a competition.	3	2	1
22.	The bigger the crowd, the more worried or tense I become.	3	2	1
23.	I have trouble focusing after an official makes a bad call against me.	3	2	1
24.	I constantly think about my performance.	3	2	1
25.	Sometimes, before a contest, I go blank.	3	2	1
	Total Score	_____		

FIGURE 10-3 WEIGHT CONTROL

Advice and Rules on Weight Control

Weight control can be seen as a favorable balance between ENERGY IN and ENERGY OUT. Anyone can lose weight by cutting down on his calorie intake (energy in) or increasing his physical activity (energy out).

The most effective way is a combination of these methods.

To lose weight safely and in moderation, a wrestler should follow these guidelines:

1. Decrease your calorie intake to 2000-2500 per day.

2. Do not attempt starvation or excessive dehydration.

3. Limit food portions at meals while maintaining proper nutrition.

4. Stay away from sauces, gravies, pastries, soda, candy, oils, ice cream and whole milk, butter, and fast foods. Restrict your salt (sodium) and sugar intake since these condiments cause ligaments and muscles to lose their suppleness and strength.

5. Eat well-balanced meals that consist of 65 percent carbohydrates (500-600 grams) and 15 percent protein. Common foods here would be pancakes, breads, potatoes, fruit, vegatables, and lean meats.

6. Drink diet pop, water, or tea.

7. Take a vitamin supplement.

8. Avoid snacking and binging, especially on the weekend after a match.

9. Do not eat past the point where your hunger is satisfied.

10. Consult the coaching staff before choosing any diet plan not mentioned here.

"Follow a diet composed predominantly of fruits, vegetables, grains, beans, and nonfat dairy products and minimize fat intake to lose weight naturally," advises Dean Ornish, MD, director of the Preventive Medicine Research Institute and author of *Eat More, Weigh Less.*

If you are constantly complaining in practice, or tired in school, or nervous about your weight, or losing your concentration in class, or irritable with others, then we must re-evaluate your selection of a weight class and review the methods you are using to lose weight. See the coaches.

FIGURE 10-4 GUIDELINES FOR EFFECTIVE WEIGHT LOSS FOR INTER-SCHOLASTIC WRESTLING

1. Avoid falling below 7 percent body fat content. Starvation occurs when a wrestler's body fat is below 6 percent.

2. Lessening calorie intake by 500 calories per day results in a two pound weight loss per week.

3. Gradual weight loss (2-3 pounds per week) helps maintain proper muscle strength.

4. Maintain a low-fat, high carbohydrate diet.

5. Protein and fat are not truly important to muscle growth. Carbohydrate and water promote muscle growth and stamina. Seventy percent of our muscles are water content.

6. An average wrestler requires a half-gram of protein for each pound he weighs. For example, a 145 pound wrestler needs about 72 grams of protein per day.

7. Wrestlers should avoid foods that lack vitamins and proteins like chips, candy, pastries, doughnuts, and sodas.

8. Better snack foods include pretzels, fruits, unsalted popcorn, fig bars, nonfat yogurt, and bagels.

9. Eating a pound of food does not always result in a pound of added weight to the body. Typically, 3500 extra calories adds one pound to a person's weight. High fat foods add more weight.

10. Fluid consumption is very important for a wrestler. If he is dehydrated at a weigh-in, he will still be dehydrated one hour later because body fluids cannot be replenished that quickly. To re-hydrate a person's body usually requires three hours.

11. Water and food restriction combined tend to weaken muscles and lessen endurance.

12. Wrestlers should drink two cups of water for each pound of weight loss. Sports drinks are more useful after a practice while cold water alone is best after a weigh-in.

13. A wrestler should be monitored carefully (record his daily weight on a chart).

14. A wrestler's parents and physician and the school's trainer should be consulted before a wrestler begins any weight loss program.

FIGURE 10-5 BEST FOODS FOR WRESTLERS

Breads/Cereals

Whole-grain cereals

Whole-grain bread

English muffins

Bagels

Plain rolls

Low-fat crackers

Brown or enriched white rice

Plain popcorn

Pretzels

Pancakes

Waffles

Meats

Lean beef or pork

Poultry without the skin

No fried meat or fish

Fish

Dairy

Skim milk

Nonfat yogurt

Nonfat cheese

Also

Fresh fruit, fresh vegetables, plain potatoes (not fried), beans, peas, and lentils

REFERENCES/BIBLIOGRAPHY

Ferguson, Howard, *The Edge*, Getting the Edge Company, Cleveland, Ohio: 1990.

Hemery, David, *The Pursuit of Sporting Excellence*, Human Kinetics Books, Champaign, Illinois: 1986.

Ogilivie, Bruce C. and Thomas A. Tutko, *Problem Athletes and How to Handle Them*, Pelham Books, San Jose, California: 1967.

Stein, Martin, "Kids and Anxiety," *NEA Today*, September 1993.

Walton, Gary, *Beyond Winning: The Timeless Wisdom of Great Philosopher Coaches*, Leisure Press, 1992.

Warren, William, *Coaching and Motivation: A Practical Guide to Maximum Performance*, Prentice-Hall, Inc., New Jersey, Englewood Cliffs: 1983.

APPENDIX

Youth/Recreation Wrestling Program Grades 2–6

BE A WINNER!

JOIN the RICHMOND HEIGHTS RECREATION DEPT.
YOUTH WRESTLING PROGRAM

For all Boys—Grades 2-6

WHEN

Every Monday and
Wednesday 6:30-8:00 P.M.

WHERE

Richmond Heights H.S.
Wrestling Room

COST

$25—Make check payable to
Richmond Heights Recreation
Department

DIRECTOR

EARLY REGISTRATION

Send checks and form to
Richmond Heights
Recreation Department
457 Richmond Road
Richmond Heights, OH 44143

LATE REGISTRATION

Between 6:00—6:30 P.M. at
first practice on Wed,
January 4

Boys will learn wrestling techniques along with tumbling, agility skills, and general body conditioning. They will also be given the opportunity to compete in matches against other youth clubs and in tournaments.

Registration Form

Name _____ Phone _____

Street Address _____

City _____ State _____ Zip _____

Date of Birth _____ Grade _____ Shirt Size _____

The undersigned assumes all risks and hazards arising out of the participation and activities of the Richmond Hts. Recreation Dept. and Richmond Hts. Board of Education and releases from liability all coaches and supervisors of the program.

PRACTICE PLANS

DAY 1

REGISTRATION

TEAM MEETING: Rules
                            Attendance
                            Practice Format
                            Encourage others to join

WARM-UP & FLEXIBILITY

AGILITY WORK: Forward rolls
                            Backward rolls
                            Bear crawl
                            Crab walk
                            Duck walk
                            Kangaroo hops

POSITION DRILLS: Bear crawl in a circle
                            Crab walk in a circle
                            Bear to crab
                            Hip heisting—Lean against partner
                            Move on knees—keep back straight
                            Shuffle in a circle

                            Move on knees—partner tries to get you off
                              balance
                            Hop overs with . . .
                              Partner flat
                              Partner in a pushup position
                              Partner on all fours

                            Bounce to stance

DAY 2

TEAM MEETING: Review rules
                            Review schedule

WARM-UP & FLEXIBILITY

AGILITY DRILLS: Forward rolls
                            Backward rolls
                            Kangaroo hops
                            Cartwheels
                            Bunny hops
                            Carioca

POSITION DRILLS:	Move on knees—left, right, forward, back
	Fix position—one knee, two knees, tripod
	Shuffle in a circle
	Tripod up with partner's leg
	Hip heist—lean against partner

TEACH:

Stance—-
Square and Staggered
Shadow wrestling

DRILLING:

Stance and Motion
Mirror wrestling—Left, right, lower, raise up
Position drill with partner

TEACH:

Illegal holds

A.   No full nelson
B.   No fingers or hands in face
C.   Cannot go against joint
D.   No punching, biting, scratching, tickling
E.   No illegal head lock
F.   No locking hands

DRILLING:

Froggy
Froggy to grabbing far arm
Froggy to grabbing far arm and near knee
Position drill—bottom man moves—top man stay
  on top—chest on back

TEACH:

How to pin
Proper alignment—Hands and head and feet
Half nelson
Reverse nelson
Breakdowns to half nelson

SITUATION:

Top man with half nelson—bottom man on back

CONDITIONING:

Play a game—Scooter/Relays

DAY 3

TEAM MEETING:

Get weights
t-shirts ordered
Bring a friend to next session

1.   Warm-up & Flexibility

2.   Agility work:

Jogging
Bunny hops
Crab

                                        Bear crawl
                                        Carioca

3.   Review: Pinning

                                        • Put branches on the log
                                        • How to stop his rolling away
                                        • How to stop his bridging off
                                        • How to tighten up a half nelson

4.   Teach: Alignment on top
                                        Spiral
                                        Breakdowns to the spiral

5.   Drilling: Position drill on top
                                        Spiral to Spiral on other side

6.   Bottom drills: Pop ups
                                        Bridging to a pop up
                                        Pop hips and cut through
                                        Hand find drill

7.   Teach: Bottom position & alignment
                                        Inside leg stand up
                                        Cut through and face off

8.   Situation Wrestling: Top man with spiral vs. bottom man on base

9.   Drilling: Stand up—circle away (no partner)
                                        Belly to base to stand up
                                        Stand up vs. partner
                                        Cut through vs. partner

10. Situation wrestling: Double leg vs. man on knees
                                        Knees vs. Knees

11. Teach: Double leg

                                        • Hands and head position
                                        • Scoot knees and hips forward
                                        • Step up and drive across
                                        • Cover down

12. Game: Mini aerobics & railroad tracks

DAY 4

1.   Warm-up & Flexibility

2.   Drilling: Back to back—stay square

Stance—touch knees
Position drill
Over/Unders
Spin drill—chest on his back
Shuffle around partner who tries to slap your legs
Mirror drill

3. Teach: Breakdowns (Spiral)

- Far arm and near knee
- Far knee and far ankle
- Tight waist and far ankle
- Tight waist and near arm

Chest on back / Control a wrist / Stay on toes
Stay on top / Keep driving into him

4. Drilling:
- Shift from side to side
- Spiral

5. Situation wrestling: Top vs. Bottom (try to pin vs. try to escape)

6. Review: How to stay off your back
Never turn into the man
How to get off butt (hip heisting)
Get to your feet (stand up)

7. Situation wrestling: Knees vs. Knees

(Have rest of group watch two boys wrestle and comment on good and bad points they observed)

8. Teach: Double leg from knees—finishes

A.   Drive across
B.   Hip out (when he posts out)
C.   Drive straight in

9. Conditioning: Relay races

DAY 5

1. Warm-up & Flexibility

2. Drilling: Pop ups against wall—Who's quickest?
Duck walks—forward and backward
Crab walk—forward and backward—side to side
Bridge off to tripod to stance

3. Teach: Scoring points

4.   Drilling: (with partner)
Move on knees—Partner pushes on shoulders
Penetration step into double leg
Inside control vs. outside control

5.   Watch video tape of match—Review how points are scored

6.   Wrestle a match—Have them keep track of their points

7.   Teach: Sprawling

- Throwing feet and knees back (from knees)
- Keep head up
- Flex legs
- Drive hips down

8.   Drilling: Sprawl from knees
Sprawl from feet
Spin drill
Keep hips square vs. angle
Sprawl and spin from knees
Sprawl and spin from feet

9.   Situation wrestling: Double vs. Sprawl

10.   Wrestle a match—keep track of points

11.   Crab soccer

DAY 6

Team Meeting: Deal with scoring system again

1.   Warm-up and Flexibility

2.   Teach: Set ups to takedowns

A.   Control his hands
B.   Inside control
C.   Fake shot to real shot
D.   Control his head—Wrist and Collar tie

3.   Drilling: Motion drill (practice set ups)
Position drill (from feet)
Review: How to "shoot"
Set ups to Double Leg attack
Set ups to Single Leg attack

4.   Teach: Sagging Headlock
–From knees

–From feet

5.   Wrestle matches

6.   Game

DAY 7

1.   Warm-up & Flexibility

2.   Relay race—Duck walk/Crab walk/Bear crawl/Sprint

3.   Position drills:

        Fix position—one knee, two knees, tripod
        Tripod and circle up with partner's leg
        Tie ups—Move partner around
        Breakdowns from top position
        Spiral

4.   Wrestle matches

5.   Review:

        Stance to Sprawl
        Partner shoots to Sprawl
        Sprawl and pull on ankles
        Sprawl and wizzer
        Snap and spin

6.   Teach:

        What to do when on butt

- vs. opponent facing you
- vs. opponent behind you

        –Turn in
        –Head wrench
        –Stand up

7.   Matches and Round Robin wrestling

8.   Game

DAY 8

1.   Team Meeting:Singlets / Competitions / Being coachable

2.   Warm-up & Flexibility

3.   Agility drills:

        Straddle jump
        Tuck jump
        Doggy walk
        Kangaroo hops

Bounce from hands to feet

4. Review: Spiral

                         How to sweep it

                         No backside spiral

                         Maintaining pressure

5. Review: Bridging

                         Bridge and turn and base

                         Bridge and turn and tripod

6. Situation wrestling: Man with half nelson vs. man on back

7. Teach: Stalled double   Stalled single

                         –stop his spin   –walk to hook leg

                         –get head outside   –reach for ankle

                         –finish opposite head
                          (head side?)

8. Matches

9. Game

DAY 9

Team Meeting:

1. Warm-up & Flexibility

2. Teach: Hip toss
                         Head-n-Arm

3. Review: Wrist ride—Control the opponent underneath
                         –hop over—side to side
                         –keep pressure on him

4. Situation wrestling—man on belly vs. man with wrist

5. Teach: Inside single
                         –to far leg Tackle

6. Matches

7. Relay races—Crab/Bear/Backward run

©1996 by Parker Publishing Company

8. Teach: Nutrition

DAY 10

Team Meeting: Upcoming matches

1. Warm up and Flexibililty

2. Agilities: Cartwheels
Round offs
Sprints

3. Review: Half nelson and Reverse nelson

Spiral from knees

4. Teach: Near leg cradle
—look for his head to be down
—position of arms
—get tight grip
—head in opponent's side
—drive forward
—chest on face and squeeze elbows

5. Drilling: Breakdowns to pin holds

6. Drilling:
• Double to half nelson
• Sprawl to spin to near leg cradle
• Stand up to outside single
• Bridge to base to stand up

7. Review: Stalled double
Stalled single

8. Matches

9. Jogging and Railroad tracks

DAY 11

1. Warm-up & Flexibility

2. Push up contest & Sit up contest

3. Review: Spiral and Pinning
• Don't get rolled
• Feet away from feet
• Chest on chest

• Near leg cradle

4.   Situation Wrestling

      A.   Pinner vs. Bridger

      B.   Spiral vs. Base

5.   Teach: Returning opponent to mat after he stands up

      A.   Safely

      B.   Never pull opponent on top of you

      C.   Heel trip forward

      D.   Heel trip back

      E.   How to maintain control

      F.   Remember to unlock hands upon return to mat

6.   Situation Wrestling

      A.   Man on knees vs. man sprawling

      B.   Man on butt vs. man behind

      C.   Man on belly vs. man with wrist

      D.   Neutral position—hand holds

7.   Matches—"King of the Mat"

8.   Mini-Aerobics session

DAY 12

1.   Warm-up & flexibility

2.   Drills: Stance—lower level—penetration step
Stance—Motion
Stance—Sprawl
Stalled inside single—tripod—circle up—tackle

3.   Matches

4.   Drill: Pop ups against wall
Crab to hip heist

Hip heist against partner
Stand ups from base position

5. Situation wrestling: Spiral vs. Base

6. Review: Getting hand control from bottom; stopping the half nelson, bridging if necessary and getting back to base

7. Review: Riding—controlling the wrist, moving from side-to-side, looking for the half nelson

8. Situation wrestling: Top vs. Bottom

9. Matches

10. Game

DAY 13

1. Team Meeting: Quad Meet, medals, uniforms

2. Warm-up & flexibility

3. Deal with common mistakes:

From Bottom:

- Get to base first
- Keep hands in front of face
- Never look back or reach back
- If on your butt, hip heist

From Top:

- Never put head over shoulder
- Stay in control by staying under the armpits
- Tightening up your half nelson
- Ride on toes, not knees
- Never ride high
- Work harder on spiral

4. Drilling: Double legs

- Drive opposite your head
- Put hands tight at his knees
- Remember set ups
- Keep moving when caught underneath

5. Matches

6. Watch: Videotape

7.   Matches

8.   Review: Near leg cradle

9.   Teach: Far leg cradle

10. Matches

11. Aerobics

RECREATION WRESTLING QUAD MATCHES

at Aurora High School
Saturday, February 20
11:00—4:00 pm

BUS DEPARTS AT 9:30 A.M.

Directions to Aurora: Take I 271 South to Rte. 422 (Solon) to
Rte. 306. Turn right off exit ramp. Stay on Rte. 306 all the way
into Aurora to West Pioneer Trail and turn right. School is on left side

&

at Cuyahoga Heights High School
Thursday, March 4
6:30—8:30 pm

BUS DEPARTS AT 5:30 P.M.

Directions to Cuyahoga Heights: 90 W to I 77 South to Grant Avenue. Turn left off
exit ramp and then turn right at next major intersection.

*Two matches for every wrestler

*Concessions will be available

*Parents' admission = $1.50

Students' admission = $1.00